I0024572

Hubert P Main, Theodore Edson Perkins

Sterling Gems

Hubert P Main, Theodore Edson Perkins

Sterling Gems

ISBN/EAN: 9783337349332

Printed in Europe, USA, Canada, Australia, Japan

Cover: Foto ©Thomas Meinert / pixelio.de

More available books at **www.hansebooks.com**

STERLING GEMS:

A COLLECTION OF

MUSIC FOR DAY SCHOOLS

AND THE HOME CIRCLE,

CONSISTING OF

SONGS, DUETS, TRIOS, CHORUSES, &c.

TOGETHER WITH A

COMPLETE MANUAL OF RUDIMENTAL INSTRUCTION.

EDITED BY
THEODORE E. PERKINS AND HUBERT P. MAIN.

New York and Chicago:
BIGLOW & MAIN, SUCCESSORS TO WM B. BRADBURY.
MAY BE ORDERED THROUGH BOOKSELLERS AND MUSIC DEALERS.

INTRODUCTION.

In offering this Manual of Instruction the authors do not claim it as wholly original.

In the fifty pages of rudimental work we have endeavored to cover every essential point, and we especially commend to the teacher's careful consideration paragraphs 23 and 24.

As the result of experience we would suggest to teachers that *they begin at the beginning.* Make the subject so plain, that it may be comprehended by everybody. Introduce every lesson by Examples that are *practical.* We have thought it wiser to insert Songs for practice in the various keys, instead of old-fashioned examples, which so soon become monotonous and tiresome. Such Songs will be found distributed throughout the body of this Work. *State every rule in as simple language as is possible,* so that it may be easily remembered. DO NOT HURRY. Progress is made more by practice than by theory. It is a good plan, when coming before the class for the first time, to sing some familiar tune, as it will serve as an introduction, and tend to do away with any embarrassment that might exist. It will be observed that we have pursued the usual course, and present the subject of Rhythmics as the starting point, but we are fully satisfied it is not necessary. The study of Melodics would be just as proper, and perhaps should come first, as *one does not speak of the length of a tone, without conceiving that it has a pitch.* The teacher will, of course, be governed in this matter by his own judgment. Especial attention is called to the foot-notes, and the teacher would do well to embody them in his explanations to the class.

In the selections, compiled and original, we have aimed to present that kind of music which will tend to build up a taste for the *true and the beautiful,* and if a few of the *rollicking songs* of the day appear among others, their presence is due entirely to the Authors' desire that neither teacher nor pupil on opening the book will find themselves entirely among strangers.

We take this opportunity to express our thanks to Dr. H. R. PALMER, Professors THEO. F. SEWARD, W. F. SHERWIN, M. L. BARTLETT, B. C. UNSELD and many others who have kindly assisted us by their contributions. We sincerely hope that STERLING GEMS may prove a valuable accessory to the teacher and a source of profit to the pupil.

THEO. E. PERKINS.

HUBERT P. MAIN.

MANUAL OF INSTRUCTION.

PARAGRAPH I.

THE ANALYSIS OF MUSICAL SOUNDS.

TEACHER says: Listen to me; and, singing a sound, about the pitch of G, asks:

1. What did you hear? A sound.

Teacher then sings two sounds, the first one long, and the second short.

2. How many sounds did I sing? Two.

3. Were they alike or different? They were different.

4. How did they differ? One was longer than the other.

5. Which was the longer, the first or last? The first.

6. Which is the shorter? The last.

Class sing a long sound, then a short one.

7. How did the first sound differ from the second? It was longer.

8. How did the second sound differ from the first? It was shorter.

TEACHER then says:

9. We have now learned that sounds may be—? Long or short.

TEACHER says: We will make a record of the fact writing the words Long or Short on the blackboard.

10. What one word expresses the distinction we have made in musical sounds? Length.

Teacher records the answer on the board opposite the words, Long or Short.

11. How do you know this distinction exists? We heard it.

The teacher may now practice the class in sections, bringing out and defining this distinction clearly.

Teacher sings two sounds, differing only in pitch, making the interval perhaps an octave, and after singing the sounds several times, asks:

12. Were the sounds I sang alike or different? Different.

Teacher sings the example again, and asks:

13. How did the first sound differ from the second? It was lower.

14. How did the second differ from the first? It was higher.

Class sing a high sound, then a low one.

15. We have now learned that sounds may be—? High or Low.

Teacher records the answer under the words, Long or Short, and says: Yes, every sound has some degree of highness or lowness, and that degree we call PITCH.

16. What did we call it? Pitch.

Teacher records the answer under the word, Length.

17. What is pitch in music? Some degree of highness or lowness of sounds.

NOTE.—We would advise the teacher not to make any effort to bring the voices to any given pitch, but leave the pupils free to express, in their own way, their ideas of high and low sounds, the only object being to bring out the distinction clearly.

18. What was the distinction we *first* made in musical sounds? They were Long or Short.

19. What *one* word expressed it? Length.

20. What was the distinction we *next* made? Highness or Lowness.

21. What *one* word expressed it? Pitch.

TEACHER says: Listen again; then singing two sounds differing only in power, asks:

22. How many sounds did I sing? Two.

23. Were *they* alike or different? Different.

24. How did they differ? One was louder than the other.

25. How did the first differ from the second? It was louder.

26. How did the second differ from the first? It was softer.

Class sing a loud sound, then a soft one.

27. We have now learned that sounds may be—? Loud or Soft.

Teacher records this answer under the words, High or Low, and says: Every sound has some degree of Loudness or Softness, and that degree we call POWER.

28. What did we call it? Power.

Teacher records the answer under the word, Pitch.

29. What is power in music? Some degree of loudness or softness of sounds.

TEACHER says: Listen again; then, singing two sounds (one may be nasal or close, the other open and free), differing in character, asks:

30. How many sounds did I sing? Two.

31 Were they alike or different? Different.

32. How did they differ? One was through the nose, the other was not.

TEACHER says: We now find that musical sounds may differ in their closeness or openness. This difference (distinguishing one voice from another), we call "Character."

Teacher records words, Closeness or Openness, under the words, Loud or Soft.

33. What do we call the difference in the (Openness) or (Closeness) of musical sounds? Character.

Teacher records the word Character, under the word Power.

34. What was the distinction we *first* found in musical sounds? They were long or short.

35. What *one* word expressed it? Length.

36. What was the distinction we *next* found? Highness or Lowness.

37. What *one* word expressed it? Pitch.

38. What was the distinction we *next* found? Loudness or Softness.

39. What *one* word expressed it? Power.

40. What was the distinction we *last* found? Closeness or Openness.

41. What *one* word expressed it? Character.

42. Can you sing a sound without some degree of Length? We can not.

43. Without some degree of Pitch? We can not.

44. Without some degree of Power? We can not.

45. Without some degree of Character? We can not.

46. Can you sing a sound without some degree of Length, Pitch, Power and Character? We can not.

47. Then how many *necessary* properties have sounds? Four.

48. Name them in order? Length, Pitch, Power and Character.

TEACHER says:

49. Since musical sounds have four necessary properties, each requiring separate study and practice, how many departments would there naturally be? Four.

50. The first department treating of what! Length.

51. The second of what? Pitch.

52. The third? Power.

53. And the fourth? Of Character.

TEACHER says: We will name the first department, RHYTHMICS.

54. What did we name it? Rhythmics.

Teacher makes a record of the name opposite the word, Length.

55. Of what does Rhythmics treat? The length of sounds.

TEACHER says: We will name the second department, MELODICS.

56. What did we name it? Melodics.

Teacher records the name opposite the word, Pitch.

57. Of what does melodics treat? The pitch of sounds.

TEACHER says: We will name the third department, DYNAMICS.

58. What did we name it? Dynamics.

Teacher records the name opposite the word, Power.

59. Of what does Dynamics treat? The power of sounds.

TEACHER says: We will name the fourth department, Quality.

60. What did we name it? Quality.*

Teacher records the name opposite the word, Character.

61. Of what does Character treat? The quality of sounds.

The black-board now presents to the class the following

TABULAR VIEW.

Distinctions.	*Properties.*	*Departments.*
Long or Short,	Length,	RHYTHMICS.
High or Low,	Pitch,	MELODICS.
Loud or Soft,	Power,	DYNAMICS.
Close or Open,	Character,	QUALITY.

* NOTE.—Quality of sound is determined by the relation of overtones to their fundamental. We may illustrate this better by comparing the tones produced by different instruments, Piano, Organ, Flute and Violin with one another. The difference between these tones is called Quality.

PARAGRAPH II.

RHYTHMICS—MEASURES.

Teacher should carefully review preceding lesson as prefatory to new subjects. Excellent review questions may be found from Nos. 34 to 61 inclusive.

Teacher may slowly count, One, two, one, two; then require the class to repeat the same.

1. How many times did you count one, two? Twice.

TEACHER says: When we count thus, we wish to divide the time into equal portions.

2. Into *what* do we divide time? Equal portions.

TEACHER says: These portions are called MEASURES.

3. What are these portions of time called? Measures.

4. What is a measure? A portion of time.

5. How many did we count for each measure? Two.

6. Then how many parts to a measure? Two.

7. Class count two measures.

While the teacher requires the class to count two measures, he sings a sound to the syllable, *la*, to each part of the second measure.

8. How many measures did you count? Two.

9. How many did I sing? One.

10. How many sounds did I sing in that measure? Two.

11. How many to each part of the measure? One.

12. What is a measure? A portion of time.

13. Now you sing the syllable *la* to each part of the first measure, and *I* will count *one, two,* then I will sing the same to each part of the second measure while *you* count, *one, two.*

NOTE.—This exercise should be repeated several times

TEACHER says: Listen, while I sing; and introduces accent, by carefully singing *la* quite loud to the first part of each measure.

14. Were the sounds of each measure alike in power? They were not.

15. Which was the stronger? The first.

Teacher says: When we sing one part of the measure stronger or louder than the other, we say that part of the measure is accented, and the other part unaccented.

16. What part of the measure is accented? The first.

17. Which unaccented? The second.

18. Sing four measures.

Teacher should quickly represent each sound successively as sung, by a dot on the board.

• • • • • • • •

19. What have I done? Made dots on the board.

20. How many did I make? Eight.

21. How many sounds did you sing? Eight.

22. The dots are made to show—? How many sounds were sung.

23. How are the sounds represented on the board? By eight dots.

24. How many sounds did you sing to each measure? Two.

25. Then how many measures did you sing? Four.

26. Where shall I place marks to separate the first measure from the second? Between the second and third dots.

27. Where to separate the second from the third? Between the fourth and fifth dots.

28. The third from the fourth? Between the sixth and seventh.

29. What do the marks indicate? The separation of measure from measure.

30. How many measures are represented? Four.

31. What is a measure? A portion of time.

32. How is it represented? By the space between the marks.

33. Can a measure be seen, heard, or must it be only represented? It must be represented.

34. How are the sounds represented? By dots.

35. What represents the division of measures? Marks.

Teacher says: Let us now change the names we have given these characters for those in common use. Dots are called NOTES.

36. What are they called? Notes.

37. What is the use of notes? They represent sounds.

Teacher says: The marks used to separate the measures from each other we call BARS.

38. What are they called? Bars.

39. What is the use of Bars? They separate the measures from each other.

Teacher says: Musical sounds are called TONES.

40. What are musical sounds called? Tones.

PARAGRAPH III.

MELODICS—THE SCALE.

REVIEW QUESTIONS FROM 31 TO 40 INCLUSIVE.

Teacher sings a sound at the Pitch of C, using the syllable La, and after repeating it several times, asks:

1. What did you hear? A tone.
2. What syllable did I use? La.
3. All may sing La as I did.

NOTE.—The teacher may request a repetition of this tone inviting at first only those who feel sure that they can sing the right tone, afterwards those who are willing to try, and finally the entire class.

TEACHER says: The tone you have learned we will name One.

4. What did we name the tone? One.
5. Sing One. Class sings.
6. What have we named One? The Tone.
7. Class listen while I sing; and when you hear a tone, other than that we have named One, you may say: New tone.

The teacher, after singing One several times, sings the next tone of the ascending series, at the sound of which the class say: New tone.

8. Was the new tone higher or lower than One? Higher.

Let the class sing One, while the teacher, alternating with them, sings the next tone of the ascending series; and after repeating this exercise several times, he asks:

9. What tone did you sing. One.
10. What tone did I sing? New tone.
11. Class, sing new tone.
12. What is the name of the first tone you sang? One.
13. What name would you naturally give to the new tone? Two.
14. All sing One to the syllable La.
15. All sing Two to the syllable La.

Teacher may now divide the class into two sections, practicing alternately One and Two.

16. How many tones have we learned to sing? Two.
17. Name them in order? One, Two.
18. Sing them in order four times.

TEACHER says: Listen, and name the tones as I sing them, but when you hear a tone other than One or Two, please say, New tone. After singing One and Two several times, the teacher finally sings the third tone of the ascending series, at the sound of which the class say, New tone, as previously directed.

19. Sing One to the syllable La.
20. Sing Two.

TEACHER sings the new tone, and says:

21. What did I sing? New tone.

Teacher should exercise the class in singing the tones promptly when he names them, and *vice versa*, naming the tones when he sings them.

22. What shall we call the new tone? Three.

The teacher, while again exercising the class in singing and naming tones, may introduce the next tone of the ascending series, which will be quickly apprehended, and named Four by the class. In a similar manner introduce tones Five, Six, Seven, and Eight, taking great care to exercise the class sufficiently to fix the tones and names in the mind.

Class should then sing the eight tones in succession, both ascending and descending. TEACHER says: This series of ascending or descending tones we will hereafter call the SCALE.

23. What did we call them? The scale.

24. Sing the scale.

25. Name the syllable we have appointed to each tone. La.

Teacher says: Instead of using the syllable la to each tone of the scale, we will hereafter apply those syllables which are in common use; for, by associating a different syllable with each tone, we shall be more likely to remember it. We will apply to the tone One, the syllable Do. (pronounced *Doh*).

26. What syllable did we apply to one? Do.

27. To what tone did we apply Do? One.

28. Sing One, and apply the syllable.

TEACHER says: To the tone *two*, we will apply the syllable *Re*. (pronounced *Ray*).

29. What syllable did we apply to Two? Re.

30. To what tone is Re applied? Two.

31. Sing One and Two, using the syllables.

TEACHER says. We will apply to the tone *three* the syllable Mi. (pronounced *Mee*).

32. To what tone did we apply Mi? Three.

33. What syllable did we apply to Three? Mi.

34. Sing One, Two and Three to the syllables we have given.

The teacher may, in the same manner, apply the remaining syllables, Fa, (pronounced *Fah*), Sol or So, (pronounced *Soh*), La, (pronounced *Lah*), Si, (pronounced *See*), and Do, to the tones Four, Five, Six, Seven and Eight. He must not be afraid of giving his class too much practice upon THIS, the most important of all exercises—THE SCALE.

35. Of what is the scale composed? Eight Tones.

36. Sing them, ascending and descending, applying the syllables.

37. What syllable did we give to the tone Four? Fa.

38. What syllable to the tone Five? Sol, or So.

NOTE.—The syllable So (pronounced Soh) is recommended instead of Sol, for the reason that it terminates with an open vowel.

39. What syllable did we give to the tone Six? La, (pronounced *Lah*).

40. To the tone Seven? Si.

41. What syllable did we give to the tones One and Eight? Do.

PARAGRAPH IV.

MELODICS—THE STAFF.

Review questions from 24 to 41 inclusive.

1. Class may sing the scale ascending and descending.

TEACHER says: As we have learned to sing the tones, with their names and syllables, we will now have some sign that will call to mind the tone to be sung.

Teacher then drawing a line on the board thus, ————————, asks:

2. What have I done? Drawn a line.

TEACHER says: Let the line represent One and the space above, Two.

3. How is One represented? By the line.

4. And what represents Two? The space above the line.

5. Class sing as I point.

NOTE.—Teacher points to the line, and the class sings the tone One to syllable Do; then to the space, when the class sings Two to syllable Re.

The TEACHER says: Listen, and if I sing incorrectly, please check me instantly by saying mistake. Teacher points and sings at the same time a few tones correctly. At length, while pointing to the line representing One, he sings Two, at the sound of which the Class says: "Mistake," as directed.

6. What tone did I sing? Two.

7. What should I have sung? One.

8. Why should I have sung One? Because the line at which you were pointing represents One.

9. Is it always necessary to represent One by the line? It is not.

Teacher says: Let the space below the line represent One.

10. If the space represents One, what will represent Two? The line.

11. How many tones of the scale have we represented? Two.

12. What are they? One and Two.

13. How many have we yet to represent? Six.

14. Name them? Three, Four, Five, Six, Seven, and Eight.

15. How did we first represent One? By the line.

16. How was Two represented? By the space above the line.

17. How shall we represent Three? Draw another line.

The Teacher draws the line and says:

18. How many tones are represented on the board Three.

19. Name them in order? One, Two, and Three.

20. One is represented by what? The first line.

21. How is Two represented By the space above the first line.

22. And Three? By the second line.

23. How shall we represent Four? By the space above the second line.

24. And Five? Draw another line.

The Teacher draws the line, and says:

25. Six shall be represented where? The space above the third line

26. And to represent Seven what must we do? Draw a fourth line.

Teacher draws the line, and says:

27. Then Eight will be represented—? By the space above the fourth line.

Teacher says: By agreement, the first line represents One, but we have found that any line or space may just as well represent One. Let One be represented by the space above the first line.

28. How is Two represented? By the second line.

29. And Three? By the space above the second line.

The Teacher may proceed thus, allowing the Class to find it necessary to still add other lines and spaces in order to represent the eight tones. Again he may commence with the second line as One, when the Class will find use for the space above the fifth line.

The board then presents the lines and spaces as follows:

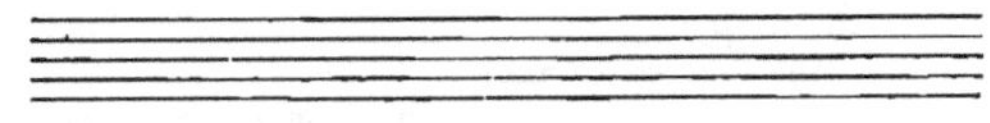

Teacher says: The lines and spaces, by which the tones are represented are called the Staff.

30. What are the lines and spaces called? The staff.

31. How many lines and spaces are there in the staff? Five lines and four spaces.

Teacher says: Each line and space of the staff we call a Degree.

32. What is each line and space of the staff called? A degree.

33. How many degrees does the staff contain? Nine.

Teacher may now point to the 1st, 3d, 5th, 3d, 4th, 2d, and 1st degrees of the staff, requesting the class to sing as he points.

On requesting them to repeat the exercise without his pointing, doubtless the result will be a failure; when it will be proper to suggest that it was forgotten on account of the imperfect system of notation that we have been using; hence, some other way than pointing must be found for preserving the order in which the tones are to be sung. The one in general use is to write a note on the line or space representing the tone to be sung.

The Teacher then writes out the exercise that was sung, thus:

No. 1.

34. What have I written upon the staff? Notes.
35. How is One represented? By the line.
36. How are all the tones represented? By the lines and spaces.
37. What represents the order in which they are to be sung? The notes.

TEACHER says: We have now found a second use for notes. They also represent the order of succession, in which tones are to be sung.

The Teacher may now represent the scale, ascending and descending.

No. 2.

Do, re, mi, fa, so, la, si, do, do, si, la, so, fa, mi, re, do.
One, two, three, four, five, six, seven, eight, eight, seven, six, five, four, three, two, one.

Class should practice it, using the names of the tones; also the syllables Do, Re, Mi, etc.

The Teacher points to the note on the first line, and asks:

38. What tone must be sung when I point to this note? One.
39. How do you know? Because the note is written on the first line.

PARAGRAPH V.

MELODICS--RELATIVE AND ABSOLUTE PITCH.

Review questions 34, 36, 30, 31, 32, 33.

1. Class sing the scale.
2. How did we represent the scale? By lines and spaces.
3. Is it necessary that we should always take the first line to represent One? It is not.
4. If the second line represents One, what represents Two? The second space.
5. How is Three represented? By the third line.
6. If the second space represents One, what represents Two? The third line.
7. What Three? The third space.

TEACHER says: Let the first line represent One.

Teacher then rubs out the upper note, and takes the line upon which the highest remaining note is written, to represent Eight.

8. Where will One now come? The space below.

Teacher again rubs out the upper note, and asks:

9. Where will One now come? You must draw another line

TEACHER says: Now, according to common usage, the staff consists of five lines and four spaces, with the space below and the one above, it is not necessarily so, only more convenient. When we find it necessary to add lines, we make them quite short, only long enough upon which to write the note. Such short lines are called ADDED LINES.

10. What are they called? Added lines.

Teacher may, in like manner, show the necessity of having added lines above the staff as well as below.

The Teacher now sings the scale, requesting the Class to name the tones as he sings them. Then, while the Class sings the scale, the teacher names them.

11. What is the name of One? One.

12. The name of Two? Two.

13. Of Three? Three.

14. In what branch of study, Geography, Arithmetic or Grammar, do we find these names? Arithmetic.

15. What are they called? The numerals.

16. What use do we make of them in music? They are the names of the tones of the scale.

17. Do their names suggest the length or pitch of sounds? The pitch.

18. Do the names suggest entire independence, or are they closely related? Closely related.

Teacher sings 1, 2, 3, 4, and requests the Class to sing 5, 6, 7, and 8.

Teacher sings 1, 2, 3, then Class sings 4, 5, 6, 7, and 8.

Teacher sings 1, 2, and Class sings 3, 4, 5, 6, 7, and 8.

Teacher sings 1, then Class sings 2, 3, 4, 5, 6, 7, and 8.

19. What tone must you have before you sing Two? One.

20. On what tone then is Two dependent? On One.

21. On what are all the tones of the scale dependent? On tone One.

TEACHER: We will therefore call One the Key-tone of the scale.

22. What did we call One? The key tone of the scale.

23. Do the tones of the scale seem independent or closely related? Closely related.

TEACHER says: The relationship that exists between the tones of the scale is called RELATIVE PITCH.

24. What is the relationship of the tones called? Relative pitch.

25. What is relative pitch? The relationship existing between the tones of the scale.

26. By what terms did we designate the relative pitch of the tones of the scale? By the numerals One, Two, Three, etc.

Teacher may now call upon the class to sing the scale, giving them the pitch of C.

NOTE.—The Teacher must be very careful not to speak of the pitch C or G at this time, as the Class are supposed to know nothing of those terms.

The Teacher then sings the scale, (pitch of G) and asks the Class.

27. How did the scale I sung differ from that you sung? In pitch.

28. May the pitch of the scale be changed? It may.

Teacher requests the Class to sing a tone two or three times, and asks:

29. Can the pitch of that tone be changed? It can not.

TEACHER says: The pitch of a tone can never be changed. It may be high or low, still it must be fixed. This essential condition of tones is called ABSOLUTE PITCH.

30. What is the essential pitch of tones called? Absolute pitch.

31. What is the relationship that exists between tones called? Relative pitch.

32. By what names is it designated? Names of the numerals.

TEACHER says: As we have names for the relative pitch of sounds, we must also have some for the absolute. The names of the first seven letters of the alphabet are taken for this purpose.

33. What are used as names for the absolute pitch of sounds? The names of the first seven letters of our alphabet.

TEACHER says: We will name the absolute pitch of the first tone C; the second, D; the third, E; fourth, F; fifth, G; sixth, A; seventh, B; and the eighth, C.

34. Name the absolute pitch of the first tone? C.

35. That of the second? D.

36. Of the third? E.

37. The fourth? F.

Teacher may call for the names of the absolute pitch of the rest of the tones of the scale.

38. What is the name of the relative pitch of the first tone of the scale? One.

39. What is the name of the absolute pitch of One? C.

40. Each tone has how many names? Two.

41. What is indicated by the names of the numerals? Relative pitch.

42. By the names of the letters? Absolute pitch.

TEACHER says: To prevent misunderstanding we will hereafter consider One, Two, Three, etc., as names indicating relative pitch, and A, B, C, etc., as indicating absolute pitch.

NOTE.—The following question is sometimes asked of the Teacher: "Why is the letter C taken in preference to A, as the name of One, in this scale, which is always presented first to the class? Answer: The tones of the minor scale received their names first and A was taken as the name for One in that scale, C, being Three of that scale, becomes One of the major. The scale based on C is often called the natural scale, but it is no more so than any other. The term natural refers only to the manner in which the scale is played on the Piano or Organ. It being the only position, in which the scale can be placed on the staff and played upon the Piano or Organ, without the use of the sharp or flat keys.

PARAGRAPH VI.

RYTHMICS—MEASURES—RESTS.

Review questions 22, 25, 32, 30, 33, 40, 41, 42.

Class counts and Teacher sings four measures.

1. How did you indicate the parts of measures? By counting.

2. Can we count and sing at the same time? We can not.

TEACHER says: We shall find it convenient to indicate the parts of measures by motions of the hand. To the first part of the measure we will give a downward motion, and to the second an upward.

3. What is the motion to the first part of the measure? Downward.

4. What to the second part? Upward.

TEACHER says: The motions of the hand, indicating the parts of measures, are called BEATS; and when we make these motions we are said to beat time.

5. Class may beat four measures.

6. How did we indicate measures to the eye? By beating.

7. How to the ear? By counting.

Teacher writes the following exercises on the board

No. 3.

TEACHER says:

8. How many measures are represented in the lesson? Four.

9. How many parts in each measure? Two.

10. What will the motions of the hand be in beating the time? Down and up.

11. What motion to the first part of the measure? Down.

12. To the second? Up.

TEACHER says:

13. Class may beat one measure then sing the exercise, beating the time while singing.

NOTE.—In order to have the motions of the hand equal, so that the division of the measure may be accurately made, let the Class describe the motions by saying, *downward beat* and *upward beat*. Let the Class in the practice of *beating time*, describe the beats *aloud*, afterwards perhaps in *a whisper*, but finally in *silence*, *thinking* only of the words that describe the beats. There is no better way of *marking the divisions* of time than by *beating*, and it should *never be discontinued*. Encourage the Class from the beginning to form the habit of *mental counting*.

TEACHER says: You may now beat the time (describing one measure before I commence), while I sing. If I do not sing the exercise correctly, say Mistake.

14. How many measures do I sing? Four.

15. How many do you count before I sing? One.

16. How many do you count altogether? Five.

Teacher sings, omitting the second tone in the last measure. Class says, "Mistake."

17. In what measure? The last.

18. What was the mistake? You did not sing the last tone.

TEACHER says: Sometimes we produce a better effect by not singing in every part of the measure so we will cancel that note.

The exercise now presents the following appearance:

No. 4.

19. How many tones do we sing in the last measure? One.

20. Class may sing the exercise.

TEACHER says: I will rub out the canceled note, and in its place write a character, signifying *silence or rest* in that part of the measure: hence the name of this character, REST.

The exercise now presents the following appearance:

No. 5.

21. What did we call the character? A rest.

22. What is a rest? A sign or mark of silence.

After practicing the Class on the exercise, restoring it to its original form, the teacher says: You may count again while I sing, and if I fail to sing the exercise as it is written, check me by saying Mistake.

No. 6.

Teacher then sings the exercise, making but one tone in the last measure, when the Class says, "Mistake."

23. In which measure? In the last.

24. What was the mistake? You sang but one tone.

25. How many tones ought I to have sung? Two.

26. Why? Because there are two represented.

The Teacher now draws a curved line over the two notes in the last measure, thus:

No. 7.

and says: Let the line unite them so that they may represent but one tone.

27. Now then (pointing to the last measure), how many tones must I sing in this measure? One.

Teacher sings the exercise and requires the class to do the same.

28. How many tones have we in regard to length? Two.

29. How did the first differ from the second? It is shorter.

30. How does the second differ from the first? It is longer.

31. What name is naturally suggested for the first? Short.

32. For the second? Long.

33. But how many *kinds* of notes have we? One.

34. Which tone does it represent? The short one.

35. How have we represented the long tone? By uniting the two notes with a curved line.

36. To represent the long tones, will it be more convenient to unite the notes with a line or make a note of a different form? Make a different note.

Teacher rubs out the two notes in the last measure. and writes One of a new form. So the exercise stands thus :

No. 8.

The Class sings the exercise again, and the Teacher asks :

37. What shall we call the notes that represent the short tones? Short notes.

38. Those that represent long tones? Long notes.

Pointing to the exercise on the board, the Teacher says :

39. How many forms of measure have we? Two.

Pointing to a measure represented by short notes, he asks :

40. Which form of measure is this, first or second? The first.

TEACHER says : We will call it the PRIMITIVE FORM of measure.

41. What did we call it? The primitive form.

42. Did we obtain the primitive form from the second or the second from the primitive? The second from the primitive.

TEACHER says : Then we will call the second a DERIVED FORM.

43. What did we call it? A derived form.

44. What did we call the first form? Primitive.

45. The second? Derived.

The Teacher may now sing first one form of measure, then the other, requiring the Class to state whether he sung primitive or derived forms.

46. Sing four measures in the following order, Primitive, Derived, Primitive, Derived.

Class sings :

Teacher may now write exercises like the following :

No. 9. No. 10.

No. 11.

Teacher, pointing to exercise No. 11, says :

47. How many measures are there in the exercise? Sixteen.

Pointing to the first measure, he asks :

48. Is this a primitive or derived form of measure? Primitive.

49. How do you know? Because there is a note in each part of the measure.

50. The second measure is it primitive or derived? Derived.

51. How do you know that? Because the two parts of the measure are united and represented by the long note.

52. How was the derived form of measure obtained from the primitive? By uniting its parts.

PARAGRAPH VII.

MELODICS—THE SCALE—CLEFS.

Review questions 6, 7, 22, 28.

1. Have we found it necessary to always represent One by the first line? We have not.

TEACHER says: For the present we will agree to represent the scale in two ways. First, in this way, commencing with the added line below:

No. 12.

Then commencing with the second space, thus:

No. 13.

Teacher, pointing to the added lines of the upper staff, asks:

2. What tone is represented here? One.

Pointing to the second space of the lower staff:

3. What tone is represented here? One.

4. How do you know that? We agreed that it should be so.

5. Is the pitch of a tone represented by the note or by the degree of the staff? By the degree of the staff.

Teacher writes a note on another staff, and asks:

6. What tone is represented here? We do not know.

7. Can some one tell me whether I wish to represent Six or One? *None can tell.*

8. If I wish to represent One on the line what figure shall I write on that line? 1.

9. Where shall I place the figure 3, in order that the first line may represent 1? On the second line.

Teacher may represent One in different places on the staff by the use of figures, as in the above example; but finally writes 5, on the second line of the upper staff, and asks:

10. Where shall we find One represented? On the added line below.

Teacher then writes 4 on the fourth line of the lower staff, and asks:

11. Where is One represented? On the second space.

TEACHER says: The figures 5 and 4 now show us where One is found, or the position of the scale upon the staff.

12. Do numerals indicate relative or absolute pitch? Relative.

13. What is the name of the absolute pitch of One? C.

14. What of Two? D.

15. The name of Three? E.

16. Of Four? F.

17. Five? G.

TEACHER says: As F and G are the names of the absolute pitch of Four and Five, to prevent confusion we will hereafter use them, instead of the figures 4 and 5, as they are used only in regard to relative pitch. Now the letters F and G tell us, that the degrees of the staff, on which they are written, represent only those tones whose absolute pitch is named G and F. When letters are used for this purpose we call them CLEFS. The word clef signifies key.

The Teacher writes the G clef, * on the upper staff, and the F clef, on the lower. Pointing to the G clef, the Teacher asks:

18. What letter is represented here? G.

Pointing to the F clef:

19. And what is represented here? F.

20. What are the letters called when thus used? Clefs.

21. How many clefs have we? Two.

22. What are their names? G and F.

23. What is the meaning of the word clef? Key.

TEACHER says: The clefs not only tell us the names of the absolute pitch of the tones, represented by the degrees upon which they are placed, but also those represented by other degrees.

24. What is the use of the clef? It determines the names of the absolute pitch of the tones represented by the degrees of the staff.

SCALES REPRESENTED BY NOTES.

No. 14. Treble Staff.
No. 15. Base Staff.
Scale-names. 1 2 3 4 5 6 7 8
Pitch-names. c d e f g a b c
Syllables. Do Re Mi Fa So La Si Do
1 2 3 4 5 6 7 8
c d e f g a b c
Do Re Mi Fa So La Si Do

No. 16. Scale Exercise. Treble Staff.
Syllables. Do Re Mi Fa So La Si Do Do Si La So Fa Mi Re Do
Scale-names. 1 2 3 4 5 6 7 8 8 7 6 5 4 3 2 1
Pitch-names. c d e f g a b c c b a g f e d c

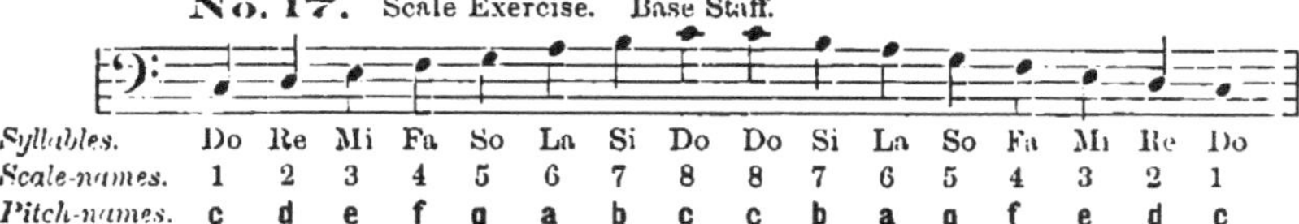
No. 17. Scale Exercise. Base Staff.
Syllables. Do Re Mi Fa So La Si Do Do Si La So Fa Mi Re Do
Scale-names. 1 2 3 4 5 6 7 8 8 7 6 5 4 3 2 1
Pitch-names. c d e f g a b c c b a g f e d c

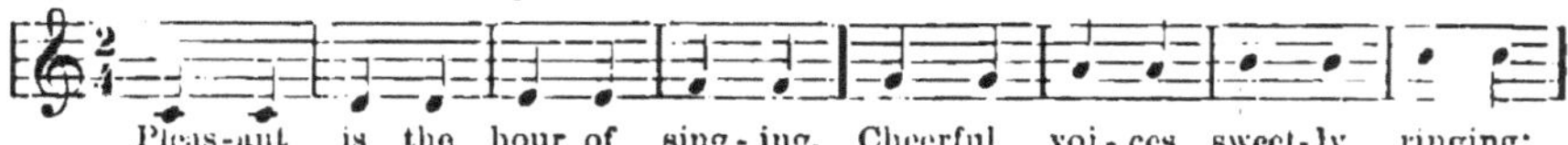
No. 18. Scale in two part measure.
Pleas-ant is the hour of sing-ing, Cheerful voi-ces sweet-ly ringing;

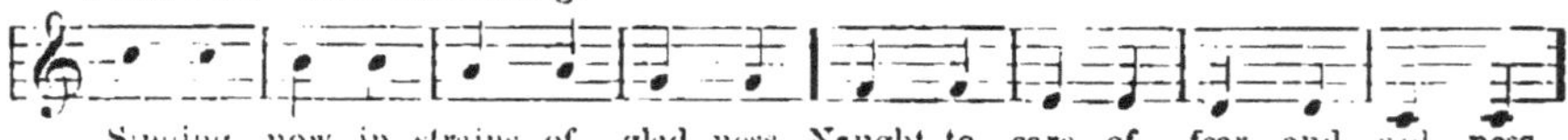
No. 19. Same descending.
Singing now in strains of glad-ness, Naught to care of fear and sad-ness.

* It will be observed that in making the G clef the final curl should go around the second line of the staff which is G; giving that name to the clef. In the F or Base clef the heavy dot with which the clef commences is always made on the fourth or F line of the staff. This clef takes its name from that line. The two dots which finish the clef, should be placed, one above and one below the line.

PARAGRAPH VIII.

RHYTHMICS—RESTS—TRIPLE MEASURES.

Review such questions as Teacher may think best.

Teacher writes the following exercise on the board:

No. 20.

After the Class practices it, he sings the same, introducing the *rest* corresponding with the long note, proceeding in a manner similar to the introduction of the short rest. Teacher need not fear of requiring too much practice of beating time.

The Teacher, calling the attention of the class, counts slowly, *one, two, three,* four times, and asks:

1. How many measures did I count? Four.
2. How many parts did I count in each measure? Three.
3. How many parts have we had heretofore in a measure? Two.
4. And we have now counted a measure with —? Three parts.
5. Class may count four measures.

Class counts.

6. How did you indicate the parts of the measure you have just counted! By counting.
7. How many ways have we of indicating the two-part measure? Two.
8. What are they? Counting and beating.
9. How have we indicated the three-part measure? By counting.

TEACHER says: We may also indicate it by beating. The motions of the hand are described, Downward beat, Hither beat, Upward beat, or down, left, up.

10. Class may beat and describe the motions of the hand through four measures.
11. How many kinds of measure have we? Two.

TEACHER says: We will call the first, the Two-part or Double Measure.

12. What did we call it? Two-part or double measure.

TEACHER says: We will call the second, Three-part or Triple Measure.

13. What did we call it? Three-part or triple measure.
14. Where does the accent fall in double measure? On the first part.

Teacher should here illustrate by counting where the accent occurs in triple measure.

15. Which part of the measure was the strongest? The first.
16. Which part was accented then? The first.
17. Which part unaccented? The second and third.

Teacher writes the following exercise on the board:

No. 21.

TEACHER asks:

18. How many measures are there in this exercise? Four.
19. How many parts in a measure? Three.
20. When a measure has three parts, what do we call it? Triple measure.
21. Class may sing the exercise.

Class sings.

22. Is the first measure primitive or derived? Primitive.

23. How do you know? Because each part is represented by a note.

24. The fourth measure, is it primitive or derived? Derived.

25. And how do you know that? Because the first and second parts are represented as united by the long note.

Teacher asks the Class to count, while he sings the exercise, but to check him if a mistake occurs. He sings but one tone in the third measure, uniting all the parts, at which the Class say, "Mistake."

26. In what measure did the mistake occur? The third.

27. What was the mistake? You sang but one tone, when you should have sung three.

28. How did the tone I sang in the third measure compare with the long tone in the second? It was longer.

29. How many parts of the third measure were united in the tone I sang? All three.

30. How many parts were united in the long tone of the second measure? Two.

31. How much longer was the tone I sang in the third measure than that of the second? One half as long again.

32. How many tones have we now obtained in regard to length? Three.

33. What was the name of the first? Short.

34. Name of the second? Long.

35. What shall we name the third? Longer.

36. How many kinds of notes have we? Two.

37. How many tones have we to represent in regard to length? Three.

Teacher says: We will represent the longer tone by a note like this:

Teacher writes the new note in the third measure, so the exercise reads thus:

No. 22.

38. How many measures are there in the exercise? Four.

39. Class sing it.

40. Is the first measure primitive or derived? Primitive.

41. How do you know it is primitive? Because each part is represented by a short note.

42. Is the second measure primitive or derived? Derived.

43. Prove it. The first and second parts are represented by the long note.

44. Is the third measure primitive or derived? Derived.

45. In what respect does it differ from the second measure? The three parts are represented by the longer note.

46. Then how many derived forms have we? Two.

47. Which parts were united to form the first derivative? First and second.

48. What parts were united in forming the second derivative? All the parts.

Teacher, pointing to the fourth measure, asks:

49. Is this measure primitive or derived? Derived.

50. Belongs to which class? The first.

51. What is a derived form of measure? The union of two or more parts of the primitive form.

Teacher writes exercise on the board as follows :

No. 23.

And requests the class to beat the time while he sings it, but to check him should he sing incorrectly.

The teacher sings the exercise, uniting the second and third parts of the third measure, when the Class check him by saying, "Mistake."

TEACHER asks :

52. Did I sing the primitive or derived form? Derived.

53. Was it the first or second derivative or a new one? It was a new one.

54. Which parts of the measure were united? The second and third.

55. With which part did the union commence? With the second part.

Teacher, pointing to the first derivative, says :

56. With which part of the measure does the union commence in the first derivative? With the first part.

57. With which part in the second? With the second.

TEACHER says : As in the first and second derivatives the union commences with the first part of the measure, we will consider them as belonging to the First Class of derivatives. And since, in the new derivative, the union commences with the second part of the measure, we will consider it as belonging to the Second Class.

The Teacher then writes in full, this table :

No. 24.
1st Derivative.
2d Derivative.

No. 25. Three part or triple measure.

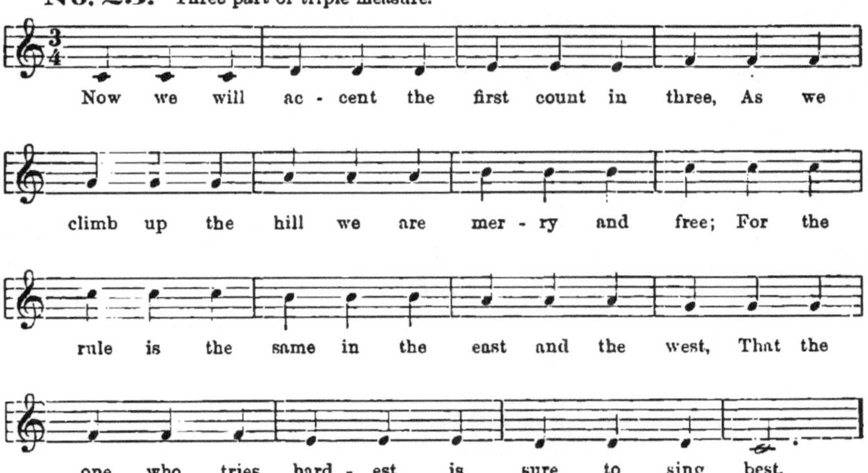
Now we will ac - cent the first count in three, As we
climb up the hill we are mer - ry and free; For the
rule is the same in the east and the west, That the
one who tries hard - est is sure to sing best.

PARAGRAPH IX.

MELODICS—INTERVALS—STEPS AND SOUNDS.

Review such questions as Teacher may think best.

After singing the scale, TEACHER says:

The difference of pitch between any two tones is called an interval. For example, the difference of pitch between One and Two, is an interval.

1. What is the difference of pitch between two tones called? An interval.

*2. What is an interval? The difference of pitch between any two tones.

TEACHER says: In the regular succession of the tones of the scale, there are two kinds of intervals, larger and smaller.

3. How many kinds of intervals are there in the scale? Two.

TEACHER says: The larger Intervals are called *Steps*, and the smaller ones *Small Steps*.

4. What are the larger ones called? Steps.

5. The smaller? Small steps.

TEACHER says: The intervals of the scale occur in the following order: Between One and Two, a step; between Two and Three, a step; between Three and Four, a small step; between Four and Five, a step; between Five and Six, a step; between Six and Seven, a step; between Seven and Eight, a small step.

NOTE.—In every Major or Diatonic scale the intervals must occur as above.

ILLUSTRATION OF THE MUSICAL LADDER.

Read from the bottom upwards.

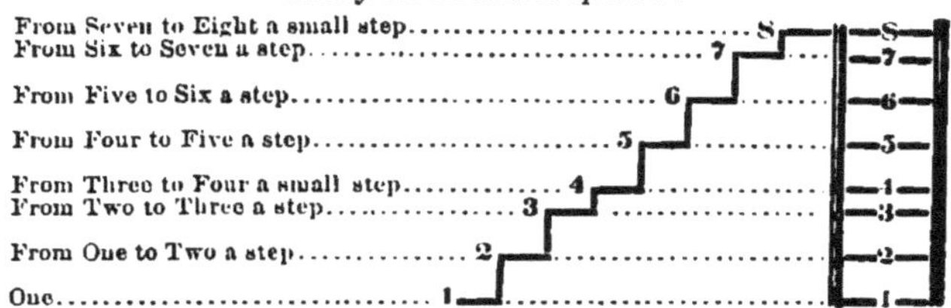
From Seven to Eight a small step
From Six to Seven a step
From Five to Six a step
From Four to Five a step
From Three to Four a small step
From Two to Three a step
From One to Two a step
One
1
2
3
4
5
6
7
8

6. How many steps are there in the scale? Five.

7. Small steps? Two.

8. What is the interval from One to Two? Step.

9. From Two to Three? Step.

10. Three to Four? Small step.

11. Four to Five, &c., through the scale.

No. 26. Interval practice. One with Five.

Do So Do So Do Do So So Do Do So So Do So Do So Do Do So So
Do Do So So Do Do So So Do Do So So Do So Do So Do.

* After the introduction of the scale, we would advise its constant practice at each and every lesson by the class; together with its various intervals commencing with the most simple of one to five; then introducing Three, &c. We assure the Teacher that a thorough knowledge of the scale (which is the foundation of every thing in music), and its various intervals, is the only means by which the pupils may acquire great facility in reading music.

No. 27. One and Five with Three.

Do So Mi Do So Mi Do So Mi So Do So Mi Do So Mi Do So Mi
Do Mi So Mi So Do So Mi Do Mi So Mi So Do So Mi Do Mi So
Do Mi So Do Mi So Do Do Mi So Do So Mi Do So Mi.

No. 28. One, Three and Five and Eight in Base Clef.

So Mi Do So Mi Do So Mi Do Mi Do Mi So
Mi Do Mi So Do So Mi Do Mi So Do So Mi Do.

No. 29. Intervals between One, Four, Six and Eight, and between Two, Four, Five and Seven.

f
1. Rustling leaves are light - ly danc - ing, Danc - ing in the breeze;
2. Gems of crys - tal clear are flash - ing, Flash - ing ra - diant light;
f
Dart - ing sunbeams bright - ly glanc - ing, Glancing through the trees.
Down the hill the brook goes dash - ing, Dash - ing on its flight.

No. 30. Rather slow, Smoothly and gently.

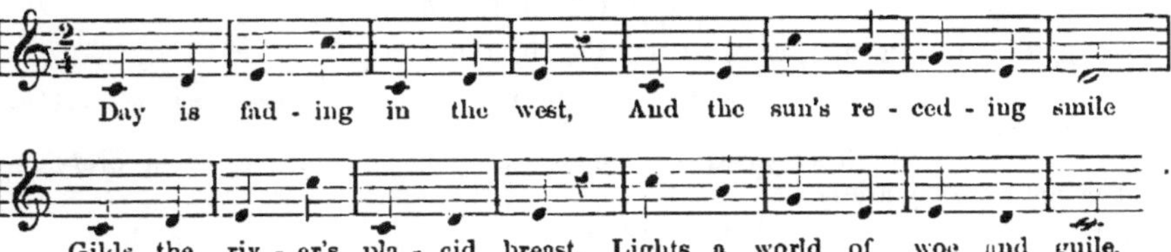
Day is fad - ing in the west, And the sun's re - ced - ing smile
Gilds the riv - er's pla - cid breast, Lights a world of woe and guile.

No. 31. Accent well.

A - rouse ye! a - rouse ye! the morn - ing is here!
The sun in the east doth so bright - ly ap - pear.

PARAGRAPH X.

THE EXTENSION OF THE SCALE.—SHARP-FOUR.

Review such questions as Teacher may think best.

TEACHER says: Please name the tones as I sing them and should you hear any other than those belonging to the scale, check me by saying, "New tone."

Teacher then sings the scale several times, both ascending and descending, at last adds the next ascending tone, at which the Class says, "New tone."

1. Was it higher or lower than Eight? Higher.
2. Some one name it? Nine.
3. Class sing Nine to the syllable La.

Teacher writes the scale thus:

No. 32.

4. Where shall I represent Nine? On the fourth line.

The tone Ten may be introduced in a similar manner, representing it on the fourth space; also the tones Eleven and Twelve.

Teacher writes the following exercise on the board:

No. 33.

And says:

5. Sing as I point.

Teacher points to the following successively:

1, 2, 2, 1, 8, 9, 9, 8, 1, 2, 3, 3, 2, 1, 8, 9, 10, 10, 9, 8,

1, 2, 3, 4, 4, 3, 2, 1, 8, 9, 10, 11, 11, 10, 9, 8.

These exercises may be extended and varied as the Class seem to require using the syllables, Do, Re, Mi, Fa, So, to Eight, Nine, Ten, Eleven, and Twelve.

6. Class think, and tell me whether these two series of tones are *alike* in every respect or not? They are not.
7. In what respect do they differ? In pitch.
8. Name the lower series? One, Two, Three, Four, and Five.

9. Name the higher? Eight, Nine, Ten, Eleven, and Twelve.

10. Again, are the two series in all respects different, or is there a similarity between them? There is a similarity.

11. What two tones in the upper series bear the same relation to each other as exists between One and Two in the lower series? Eight and Nine.

12. What corresponds with One of the lower series? Eight.

13. What tone with Two in the lower? Nine.

14. In what respect are the two series alike? In their relation to each other.

15. How do they differ? In pitch.

TEACHER says: The relative pitch of these two series of tones is the same, but the absolute is not. We regard the upper series as the same scale relatively, though at a higher pitch.

16. What tone of the upper series is also Eight of the lower? One.

17. What tone of the lower is also One of the upper? Eight.

The extended scale may now be represented thus:

No. 34.

Teacher should state that the pitch of the three upper tones represented are beyond an easy compass of the voice. Perhaps it might be well to try them once in order to convince them of the fact.

TEACHER says: We will name the upper series as One above, Two above, Three above, etc.

18. What are they named? One above, Two above, Three above, etc.

The extension of the scale downward may be brought out in the same manner, naming the tones as Seven below, Six below, etc.

TEACHER says: We have now, when considered in respect to *absolute* pitch, *three* scales, but in respect to *relative* pitch we have only *one*.

Teacher sings the scale, then requires the Class to do so two or three times, and says:

19. Name the tones I sing, and if you hear one that does not belong to the scale say, "New tone."

Teacher then sings, One, Two, Three, Four and Five, several times, in any order; finally introduces Sharp-four, when the Class says, "New tone."

20. Does it seem to be higher or lower than Five? Lower.

21. Higher or lower than Four? Higher.

Teacher may now exercise the Class as follows: Class sings One, Two, Three, Four and Five; Teacher sings Sharp-four. Class sings Five; Teacher sings Sharp-four; and finally Class sings Sharp-four and Five.

TEACHER says: We have now found a new tone existing between Four and Five, and when we speak of it we do so in relation to Four; therefore the name given it is Sharp-four.

22. What is the name of the new tone? Sharp-four.

23. Where do we represent Four? On the first space.

TEACHER says: We are allowed to represent the new tone by the same degree that represents Four if we write this (♯) character or sign before the note. We call this character a SHARP.

24. What do we call it? A sharp.

NOTE.—The term sharp, as used in music, signifies higher.

TEACHER says: We sometimes wish the space to represent Sharp-four, and indicate it by writing the sharp upon it.

25. What is the effect of the sharp? It makes the space represent Sharp-four instead of Four.

26. Has the sharp any effect on the note? None.

27. Can we sharp Four? We can not.

Teacher may have the class sing Four, Sharp-four and Five several times, then separating them in two sections have them name the tones, and sing them alternately.

28. Can you raise Four to Sharp-four? We can not.

Teacher writes the following exercise upon the board:

No. 34.

After having been sung, the class should be questioned in regard to the Rhythmic as well as the Melodic construction of exercises, for instance: How many measures are there in the exercise? What kind of measure is it? What is a measure of two parts called? How many measures are in primitive form? How many in derived? Where is the accent in double measure? What is the name of the new tone introduced? In what measure does it occur? How do we know that we are to use Sharp-four in those measures, etc?

Teacher then says: A sharp continues its effect through the measure in which it occurs.

29. How long does the effect of a sharp continue? Through the measure in which it occurs.

PARAGRAPH XI.

QUADRUPLE MEASURE—NAME OF NOTES AND RESTS.

Review such questions as Teacher may think best.

Teacher counts *one, two, three, four,* three times.

1. How many measures did I count? Three.
2. How many parts in each measure? Four.
3. How many kinds of measures have we had before? Two.
4. Name the first variety? Double measure.
5. The second? Triple measure.

TEACHER says: The kind now obtained we will call Quadruple Measure.

6. What did we call it? Quadruple measure.
7. How many parts has a double measure? Two.
8. A triple has how many? Three.
9. And a quadruple measure? Four.
10. Class may count two quadruple measures.
11. How do we indicate the parts of measure to the eye? By beating time.

TEACHER asks: In quadruple measure there are four motions of the hand—Downward beat, Thither beat, Hither beat, Upward beat, or down, left, right, up, are the terms used in describing them.

12. How many motions are there in quadruple measure? Four.
13. Describe them? Down, left, right, up.
14. Where is the accent in double and triple measure? On the first part of the measure.

TEACHER says: In quadruple measure we have two accents, as in the words *secondary, momentary.* The first, which is the stronger, and occurs on the first part of the measure, is called Primary. The second, less strong, occurring on the third part of the measure, is called Secondary.

15. How many accents are there in quadruple measure? Two.

16. Where do they occur? On the first and third parts of the measure.
17. Name of the first accent? Primary.
18. Of the second? Secondary.
19. Which is the stronger The primary.
20. The weaker? The secondary.

Teacher writes the following exercise on the board:

No. 35.

21. How many measures have I represented in the exercise? Three.
22. What kind of a measure? Quadruple.
23. How many parts in a quadruple measure? Four.
24. Are these measures in primitive or derived form? Primitive.
25. Why? Because each part is represented by a note.
26. Class may sing the exercise.

Teacher writes the first derivative under the first measure, and asks:

27. What form have I written? Derived.
28. What derivative? The first.
29. Which class? The first.
30. Class sing it.
31. What parts are united in this derivative The first and second.
32. How shall I complete the measure? By two short notes.

Exercise stands:

No. 36.

33. Which parts of the measure are united in the second derivative? The first, second and third.
34. What note shall I write? A longer note.
35. How shall I fill the measures? With a short note.

Exercise stands:

No. 37.

Teacher may now introduce, in the same manner, all the other derivatives, practicing the Class upon each one in succession; finally he sings one tone to the measure, while the Class beats the time for him, and asks:

36. How many tones did I sing in the last measure? One.
37. How did it compare in length with the other? It is the longest.
38. What shall we name this tone? Longest.
39. Have we a character to represent it? We have not.

Teacher writes this (𝅝) upon the board under the derivative of the first class, and pointing to it, says: Let this note represent the longest tone.

40. How many tones have we now in regard to length? Four.

41. And how many forms of notes? Four.

42. Name them? Short, long, longer, and longest.

TEACHER asks, pointing to the notes upon the board:

43. How does the short tone compare with the longest in length? It is only one-quarter as long.

44. What is the proportionate length of the long note? One-half.

45. The proportionate length of the longer note? Three-quarters.

TEACHER says: Then we will adopt these fractional terms as descriptive of the relative length of these tones, and also as names for the notes representing them.

46. What will be the name of the short note? Quarter-note.

47. What of the long note? Half-note.

48. And the longer one? Three-quarter-note.

49. The longest one? Whole-note.

Teacher now proceeds to draw out the derived forms of both the second and third classes, the detail of which it seems unnecessary to present here. The result will be a tabular view, as follows:

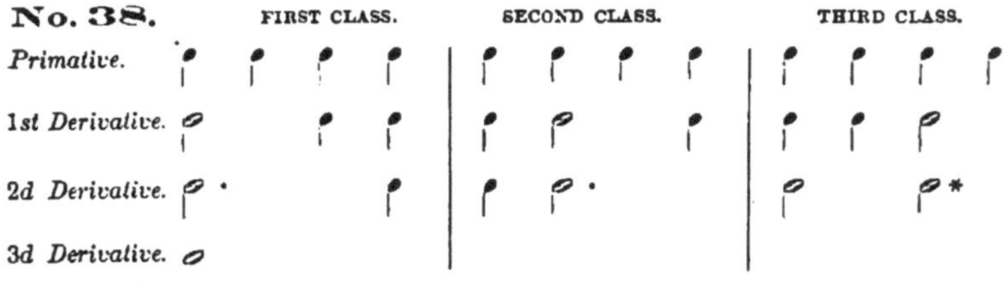
No. 38.
FIRST CLASS.
SECOND CLASS.
THIRD CLASS.
Primative.
1st Derivative.
2d Derivative.
3d Derivative.
*

We presume it to be quite unnecessary to illustrate the manner of introducing the rests that correspond to the several notes, as the principle has previously been shown, and well understood by the Class. In the following table are given the signs as used, with their names:

Quarter Note Rest. *Half Note Rest.* *Three-quarters or Dotted Half Note Rest.* *Whole Note Rest.*

No. 39. Exercises in Intervals.

Do Do Si Re Do So So Si Re So Si Re So Si Re Si Do So

So Si Re Si Do So Re Si Do So Re Si Do So Re Si Do So Mi Do.

---

* IRREGULAR. The second derivative in the third class belongs perhaps equally to the first and third classes, as the union commences on the first as well as on the third parts of the measure. We place it in the third class, and call it IRREGULAR.

No. 40.

Do Do Si So Si Re Do Re So Re So Re Si Re Do

Re Si Re Si Do Mi So Re So Re So So Si Re Do

So Si Re Do So Si Re Do Re So Si Re Do.

No. 41.

Do Re Si Do Re Si Do So Mi Re Re Mi Fa La Re

So Do Si Re Do So Si Re Do So Mi

Fa So Mi Fa Re Mi Fa La So Fa La Re So Do Si Re Do.

PARAGRAPH XII.

RHYTHMICS—SEXTUPLE MEASURE—VARIETIES OF MEASURE.

Review such questions as Teacher may think best.

NOTE.—The Teacher may refer to the lessons where Triple and Quadruple measures are introduced, as limited space will not permit the further giving of Questions and Answers in this department.

1. A measure having six parts with *primary* accent on the *first* part, and *secondary* accent on the *fourth* part, is called *Sextuple measure.* We represent it as follows.

No. 42.

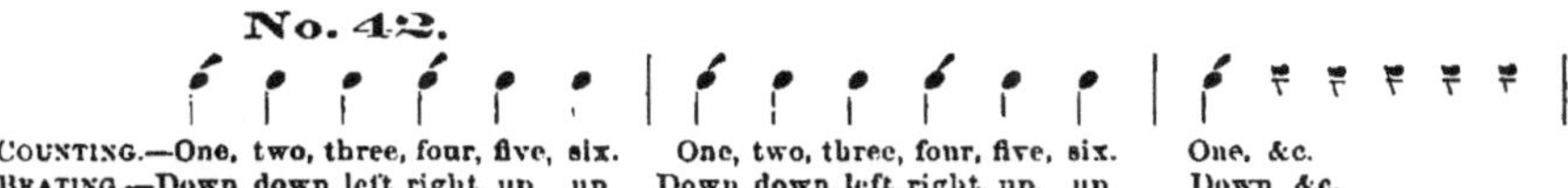
COUNTING.—One, two, three, four, five, six. One, two, three, four, five, six. One, &c.
BEATING.—Down, down, left, right, up, up. Down, down, left, right, up, up. Down, &c.

2. There may be as many varieties in all the different kinds of measure as there are kinds of notes.

3. The movement of a tune, whether, fast or slow, does not depend on the kind of notes used, for they represent only relative length.

4. Figures are used to indicate the *kinds* of measure, and also to distinguish the *varieties* of measure. When used for both purposes, the two figures are written as in the representation of fractions, the number of parts, on which the *kind of measure* depends, being indicated by the numerator : and the kind of notes used in each part, on which the *variety of measure* depends, being indicated by the denominator.

No. 43.
2/1 3/2 4/2 6/2
2/2 3/4 4/4 6/4
2/4 3/8 4/8 6/8
2/8 3/16 9/8 12/8

5. SYNCOPE. When a tune commences on an *unaccented* part of a measure, and is continued on an *accented* part of a measure, the accent is inverted ; such a tone is called a SYNCOPE, or a SYNCOPATED TONE, and the note representing it is called a SYNCOPATED NOTE. See Exercise No. 44.

NOTE 1.—Syncope, from two Greek words, signifying "to cut into," or "to cut off." A syncope cuts into, or breaks up, or contradicts the regular order of accent.

NOTE 2.—While it is important that rhythmic accent should be observed, its constant mechanical or drum-like recurrence is stiff, ungraceful, and repulsive to good taste. Such an accent belongs mostly to music of an inferior character, or to that which makes its appeal to the more external sense. Rhetorical accent or emphasis, or that which belongs to emotion, expression, or to poetical thoughts or ideas, on the contrary, is essential to a tasteful or appropriate performance, and should receive much attention. The common rules for accent are therefore liable to many exceptions.

No. 44.

Do Do Re Re Re Mi Mi Mi Fa Fa Fa So So So La La La Si Si Si Do Do

Do Do Si Si Si La La La So So So Fa Fa Fa Mi Mi Mi Re Re Re Do Do.

6. Vertical lines (as in the foregoing examples) are used to mark the boundaries of measures in notation ; they are called BARS.

7. The end of a section or period, or the final close of a piece of music, or the end of a line in poetry, is often indicated (as at the close of the foregoing examples) by a DOUBLE BAR.

PARAGRAPH XIII.

TRANSPOSITION BY FIFTHS.

Review such questions as Teacher may think best.

Teacher sings the scale, and requests the Class to sing the same.

Also sings Five, then the Class the same.

1. Class sing Four, Sharp-four, and Five to the syllable La.

2. Class sing One.

3. What is the name of the tone you sang? One.

4. What syllable do you apply to One? Do.

5. What syllable have we applied to Four? Fa.

Class sings One, Two, Three Four, as called for.

Teacher sings Sharp-four and asks:

6. What tone did I sing? Sharp-four.

7. Have we any syllable for Sharp-four? We have not.

TEACHER says: The syllable commonly used is called Fi. (Pronounced *Fee*).

Class may now practice the following exercise, using the syllables:

1	2	3	4	5	6	♯4	5.		
5	♯4	5			2	3	♯4	5.	
3	♯4	5			5	♯4	3	2.	

NOTE.—We have found it advisable to give the example before asking the Class to sing.

Teacher sings Sol, Fi, Mi, Re, and Class repeat the same. Teacher again sings, using the syllables Do, Si, La, Sol, Class sings the exercise after him; he then writes it on the board, and finishes the scale, using the Syllables Fa, Mi, Re, Do.

Class sings the exercise after the teacher, applying the syllables Do, Si, La, etc., both up and down.

8. What do you call this succession of tones? The scale.

9. What is the pitch of One in this scale? G.

Teacher sings the scale of C, Class repeats the same. Teacher then asks:

10. What is the pitch of One in this scale? C.

11. Class may sing the scale commencing with C.

12. The scale commencing with G.

TEACHER says: Where any other starting point than C is taken, the scale is said to be transposed.

13. When is the scale transposed? When another starting point than C, is taken as One.

Teacher sings the scale of G, using F, instead of F♯.

14. Did it sound right? It did not.

15. Class sing the scale of G.

16. Name the tones in the scale of G. G, A, B, C, D, E, F♯, G.

17. Class sing the scale of C.

18. Name the tones in the scale of C. C, D, E, F, G, A, B, C.

19. What tone do we use in C that we do not in G? F.

20. What in G that we do not in C? F♯.*

21. Class sing first the scale of G, then C.

22. What is the difference between these scales? They differ in pitch.

TEACHER says: The changing of the pitch of the scale is called transposition.

23. What is it called? Transposition.

24. When we take C as One of the scale, in what key are we said to sing? The key of C.

* NOTE.—The pupil may ask the question, why F♯ is used. Answer. In the key of C there are no flats and sharps used in playing that scale on the Piano or Organ. While in the key of G, in order to preserve the same order of intervals as occur in the key of C, the tone F♯ is used instead of F.

25. When G is taken as One in what key do we sing? In G.

TEACHER says: The key is used to denote relationship: C is the father of that scale; G is the father of *that* scale.

26. Tell me the names of the family of G. G, A, B, C, D, E, F♯, G.

27. The names of the family of C. C, D, E, F, G, A, B, C.

28. What tone do we use in G that we do not in D? F♯.

29. How is it represented? By placing the character called a sharp before the note on the degree of the staff which represents F.

TEACHER says: When we write music in the key of G, we place this (♯) character immediately after the clef, which does away away with the necessity of repeating it every time we use F♯.

30. What is the sign that we are singing in the key of G? The sharp placed after the clef.

No. 16. Scale of G. Treble or G Clef.
No. 17. Scale of G. Base Clef.
No. 18. Round. In Four Parts.
1
Hail to the month, to the cheering month of May,
2
Now to the woods, to the woods a - way!
3
Hear the mer - ry war - blers on the spray, We will
4
all be as hap - py, as hap - py as they.

NOTE.—Transposition affects the instrument only. The scale is the same to the singer, with its various intervals, no matter what the pitch may be. If the teacher has given his pupils practice in the scale of C with its various intervals, the bugbear of transposition will vanish, for it is the same to the voice whether pitched high or low.

PARAGRAPH XIV.

SECOND TRANSPOSITION BY FIFTHS.

Review such questions as Teacher may think best.

TEACHER says: Where any other starting point than C is taken, the scale is said to be transposed.

1. What other starting point than C have we taken? G.

2. Class sing scale of G.

3. When we transposed the scale to G, how far did we move it? Up to Five.

TEACHER says: The interval or distance from One to Five is called a Fifth.

4. What is it called? A Fifth.

TEACHER says: When we take G as the starting point for the new scale, we are said to transpose the scale a Fifth.

5. What tone do we sing in the key of G, which we do not sing in the key of C? F♯.

6. How does the pitch of F-sharp differ from F? It is higher.

Teacher says: In order that the same succession of intervals may be preserved in the scale of G as in C, we use the tone of F♯ instead of F.

7. What new tone do we use? F♯.

8. What is the scale name of F♯ in the scale of C? Sharp-four.

9. What is the name in the scale of G? Seven.

Teacher says: Whenever we transpose the scale a Fifth, we shall find that we sing one new tone; hence this Rule: *Sharp-four transposes the scale a fifth.*

Class sing 1, 2, 3, 4, 5, scale of G.

10. What number of the scale was the last tone which we sang? Five.

11. What was its pitch? D.

12. Sing this tone to syllable Do, and think of it as One.

Class sing.

13. Do you think we can sing the whole eight tones of the scale above this? No.

14. Think of this tone as Eight, and sing down to the lower D?

No. 49.

Do Si La Sol Fa Mi Re Do.

Teacher says: We will represent one of the scale on this lower D, as we cannot sing it above.

Teacher have class practice scale up and down.

15. How does this scale differ from the scale of C? The pitch.

16. How from the scale of G? In pitch.

17. Is there any difference in the manner of singing the two scales? There is not.

Class sing scale of D.

Teacher says: According to our rule, we must have sung a new tone, which we did not have in the scale of G.

18. Do you know what new tone you sang according to the rule? Yes.

19. What was it? We sang sharp-four in G instead of Four.

20. What was the pitch of Four in the key of G? C.

21. What the pitch of sharp-four? C-sharp.

Teacher says: Under our rule we must have sung C-sharp instead of C, when we sang the scale of D.

22. What is C-sharp in the scale of D? Seven.

Teacher says: Now as we sing the tones of F♯ and C♯, when D is taken as one, F♯ and C♯ (or two sharps), are called the signatures or signs of the key of D, and are placed upon the F line and space C, as in example.

No. 50. Scale in Key of D.

Do Re Mi Fa Sol La Si Do
1 2 3 4 5 6 7 8
d e f♯ g a b c♯ d
d e f♯ g a b c♯ d

23. When we moved the scale from the pitch C to G, how far did we transpose it? A fifth.

24. When we went from the pitch of G to D, how far did we transpose it? A fifth.

25. When we transpose a fifth, how many new tones do we sing? One.

26. What rules have we about the new tones in transposing? Sharp-four transposes the scale a fifth.

27. What new tone did we sing when we transposed from C to G? F-sharp.

28. What number of the scale is F-sharp, in the key of C? Sharp-four.

29. What new tone did we sing when we went from G to D? C-sharp.

30. What number of the scale is C-sharp, in the key of G? Sharp-four.

31. What is the signature of the key of G? One-sharp (F-sharp).

32. What is the signature of the key of D? Two sharps (F-sharp and C-sharp).

NOTE FOR TEACHER.—Further illustrations on this subject will not be necessary, since the principle is the same in each succeeding transposition. So we merely mention the transpositions.

33. *Third transposition by Fifths: from D to A.* In this transposition G (Four) must be omitted, and G♯ (Sharp-four) must be taken as Seven to A.

No. 51. Scale of A. Three Sharps, F, C and G.

No. 52. Another form of the Scale of A.

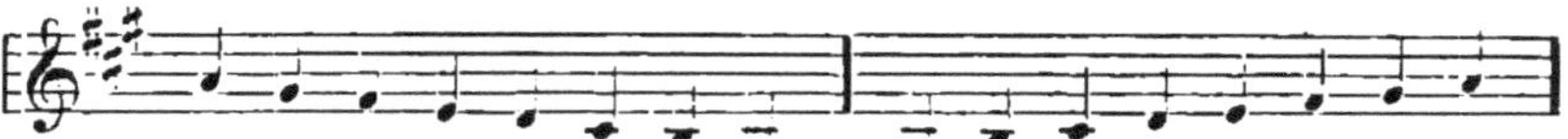

34. *Fourth transposition by Fifths; from A to E.* In this transposition D (Four) must be omitted, and D♯ (Sharp-four) must be taken as Seven to E.

No. 53. Scale in Key of E.

Do Re Mi Fa Sol La Si Do
1 2 3 4 5 6 7 8
e f♯ g♯ a b c♯ d♯ e
e f♯ g♯ a b c♯ d♯ e

NOTE.—Although we proceed briefly to point out further transpositions by fifths, yet they will not be needed for the common purpose of vocal class-teaching.

35. *Fifth transposition by Fifths; from E to B.* A must be omitted and A♯ taken.

36. *Sixth transposition by Fifths; from B to F♯.* E must be omitted and E♯ taken.

37. *Seventh transposition by Fifths; from F♯ to C♯.* B must be omitted and B♯ taken.

38. *Eighth transposition by Fifths; from C♯ to G♯.* F♯ must be omitted and F Double-sharp (F×) taken.

39. The scale may be still further transposed by fifths: to the key of D𝄪, with nine sharps (two double-sharps); to the key of A𝄪, with ten sharps (three double-sharps); to the key of E𝄪, with eleven sharps (four double-sharps); to the key of B𝄪, with twelve sharps (five double-sharps), and so on.

NOTE 1.—The key of B♯ is the same to the ear as the key of C. The differance is not in the thing itself but merely in the written signs, or notation.

NOTE 2.—The keys beyond F♯ (six sharps) are but seldom used, as the same variety may be more easily obtained in transposition by fourths. The keys beyond E (four sharps) are seldom used in common vocal music.

40. It will be observed, that in each of the foregoing transpositions the pitch has been removed a *fifth;* and that the intermediate tone required to preserve the identity of the scale in the new key has been *Sharp-four;* hence the following rule: "*Sharp-four* transposes the scale a *fifth;*" or, "The tone of transposition between any key and that which is based on its fifth, is *Sharp-four.*"

PARAGRAPH XV.

MELODICS—RHYTHMICS—FLAT-SEVEN—NATURAL—DIVIDED FORMS OF MEASURES.

Review such questions as Teacher may think best.

Under direction of the teacher the Class sings the scale two or three times. Teacher then says:

1. You may name the tones I sing, and if you hear one that does not belong to the scale say, "New Tone."

Teacher then sings the scale, repeating the tones 5, 6, 7 and 8, once or twice in any order he may please, and finally introduces Flat-seven, at which the class says, "New Tone."

2. Does the new tone seem to be higher or lower than Seven? Lower.

3. Higher or lower than Six? Higher.

TEACHER says: When used in connection with Seven, we call it Flat-seven.

4. What do we call the new tone? Flat-seven.

The Teacher may here exercise the class in a manner similar to that used in the introduction of Sharp-four, and then write exercises on the board similar to the following:

No. 54.

Teacher should question the Class in regard to the key in which the exercise is written, the kind of measure, the form of measure, whether primitive or derived, and in regard to the tones that do not belong to the scale of C.

Teacher writes the folllowing exercise on the board:

No. 55.

and requests the Class to sing it two or three times, after which he says: Listen to me; and if I do not sing the exercise as written, check me by saying, "Mistake."

Teacher sings the exercise once or twice correctly, and then purposely sings F in the second measure instead of F♯. Class says, "Mistake."

Teacher says: I wish you to sing F instead of F♯, and in order that you may know it, I will write this character (♮), which is called a *Natural*, before the note.

5. What name is given this character? Natural.*

Teacher says: The natural cancels the effect of the sharp or flat.

6. What is the effect of the natural? It cancels the effect of the sharp or flat.

Teacher says:

7. Count four two-part measures, while I sing, and see what form of measure I use in singing, whether primitive or derived.

Teacher, using syllable La, sings first and third measures in primitive form, and second and fourth in derived; then asks:

8. Was the first measure primitive or derived? Primitive.

9. Second—primitive or derived? Derived.

10. In what form was the third? Primitive.

11. And the fourth? Derived.

12. Class count again.

Teacher sings two sounds to each beat in the third measure, and asks:

13. Was the third measure like either of the others or different? It was different

14. How many La's were sung in the first measure? Two.

15. How many in the third? Four.

16. How many to each part of the measure? Two.

Teacher says: We will represent the exercise in this way:

No. 56.

17. How many tones are represented in the first measure? Two.

18. What kind of measure do you call it? Two-part or double measure.

19. What form of measure? Primitive.

20. What form is the second measure? Derived.

21. The third measure has how many notes to each part of the measure? Two.

Teacher says: We call these Divided Parts of Measure.

22. What do we call them? Divided parts of measure.

Teacher says: When we have two notes on each part of the measure it is called a compound measure.

23. What is it called? A compound measure.

Teacher says: When there is one tone on each part of the measure it is called a simple measure,

24. What is it called? A simple measure.

Teacher then writes a table of primitive form of compound measure, with derivatives, as follows:

No. 57.

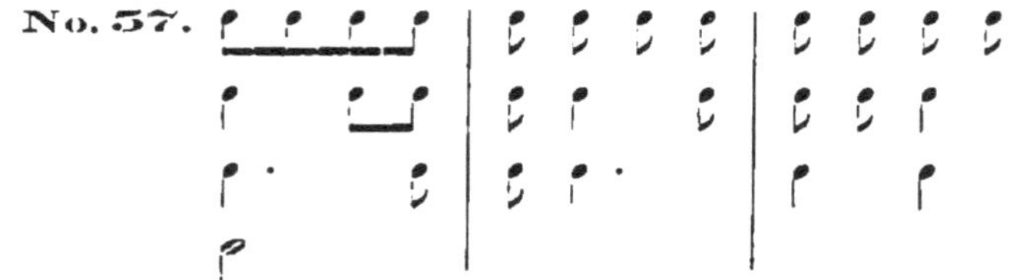

Teacher says:

25. Have we ever had this form of measure before? We have.

* We do not like the term natural as here used, as F♯ is just as natural to the ear as F. Restoral, nulifier or cancel would be more consistent.

26. We will then erase them, though they are derivatives of this form of measure.

Teacher then writes an exercise, introducing the new note, as follows :

No. 58.

and gives it the name of Eighth Note.

PARAGRAPH XVI.

MELODICS—TRANSPOSITION OF THE SCALE BY FOURTHS.*

Review such questions as Teacher may think best.

1. TEACHER. In all our transposing thus far, we moved the scale each time, what distance? A fifth.

2. Each time we transposed the scale a fifth we used how many new tones? One.

3. What new tone did we use? Sharp-four in the place of four.

TEACHER says: Suppose we try the experiment of transposing the scale a fourth instead of a fifth, as heretofore.

4. First, we will all sing the scale in the key of C.

Teacher and class sing the scale in the key of C.

5. Now we will sing up to four of the scale, and then stop.

All sing up to four.

6. What pitch is four of the scale in the key of C? F.

TEACHER says. Very well; now we will take the pitch F for One.

7. All sing it to the syllable Do.

All sing.

8. Now all sing with me the scale up and down, taking the pitch F for One

All sing.

Teacher will write scale out on the board.

No. 59. Scale in Key of F.

Do Re Mi Fa So La Si Do
1 2 3 4 5 6 7 8
f g a b♭ c d e f
f g a b♭ c d e f

* NOTE.—The reason why the scale is transposed by fifths or by fourths, is this: those keys which are based on Five or Four of any given key are its most nearly related keys. Any key, and the key which is based upon its fifths, have all their tones but one in common. Thus to the key of C belong all the tones that belong to the key of G, with the exception of F-sharp; and to the key of G, belong all the tones which belong to the key of C, with the exception of F; hence the near relation between the two keys. Again, the same is true of any key, and the key which is based on its fourth. The key of C and F, for example, have all their tones in common with a single exception. Hence the near relation.

9. To preserve the proper order of intervals between Three and Four, and between Four and Five in this transposition, it is necessary to take B♭ as four in the new key. B♭ is, therefore, the signature to the Key of F.

No. 60. Illustration.

Step, step, small step, step, step, small step, step, step, step, small step, step,
One, Two, Three, Four, Five, Six, Seven, Eight, Two, Three, Four.
One, Two, Three, Four, Five, Six, Seven, Eight.

TEACHER says: As we always sing the pitch B-flat when F is taken for One, B-flat is said to be the signature to the key of F.

10. How far have we transposed the scale now? A fourth.
11. How many new tones were we obliged to use? One.
12. What was that? B-flat.
13. How does B-flat differ from B? It is lower.*
14. What then is the signature or sign to the key of F? One-flat on the third line.
15. In what key is the following tune written? etc? In F.

No. 61. KEEP TO THE WORK YOU BEST CAN DO. Round.

1
2
Keep to the work you best can do, And let all oth - er business go.

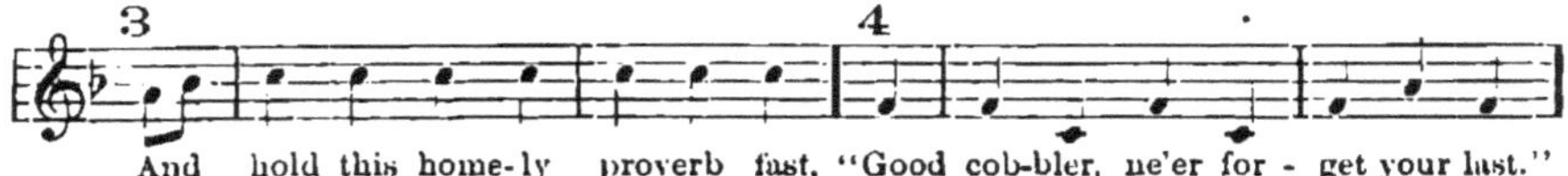
3
4
And hold this home-ly proverb fast, "Good cob-bler, ne'er for - get your last."

TEACHER says: It will be observed that, in the foregoing transposition from C to F, the pitch of the scale has been removed a *fourth;* and the intermediate tone, B♭, or *Flat-seven,* has been found necessary to preserve the proper order of the intervals. Hence the following rule: "*Flat-seven* transposes the scale a fourth;" or, "The tone of transposition, between any key and its fourth, is *Flat-seven.*"

PARAGRAPH XVII.

SECOND TRANSPOSITION BY FOURTHS.

Review such questions as Teacher may think best.

1. In our last transposition, how far did we move the scale? A fourth.
2. We found that we sang what new tone? B-flat in the place of B.
3. What number of the scale is the tone B in the key of C? Seven.

* FLAT, in musical language, means *lower;* B-flat, a half-step lower than B.

TEACHER says: And when we transposed to F (a fourth), we substituted flat-seven for Seven. We will find that whenever we move the scale a fourth we shall be obliged to substitute flat-seven for Seven in the old scale. Hence this:

RULE: Flat-seven transposes the scale a fourth.

TEACHER says: We will now transpose the scale again, following this rule.

4. What pitch is Four in the key of F? B-flat.

TEACHER says: We will take this tone B-flat for One. But in order to do this according to our rule we must substitute flat-seven for seven of the Key of F, which becomes four of the new scale.

5. What pitch is Seven in the key of F? E.

6. Then, when we transpose, in the place of E, or Seven, we shall sing what? E-flat, or flat-seven.

7. Then when B-flat is taken for One, how many flats will we have? Two.

8. What will they be? B-flat and E-flat.

9. What, then, is the signature to the Key of B-flat? B-flat and E-flat, or two flats.

No. 62. Scale in Key of B-Flat.

Do Re Mi Fa So La Si Do
1 2 3 4 5 6 7 8
b♭ c d e♭ f g a b♭
b♭ c d e♭ f g a b♭

10. What is the rule for transposing when we move the scale a fourth? Flat-seven transposes the scale a fourth.

11. What is the rule when we move the scale a fifth? "Sharp-four," etc.

12. How far did we transpose when we went from C to F? A fourth.

13. What is the signature to the key of F? One-flat.

14. How far did we transpose when we went from F to B-flat? A fourth.

15. What is the signature to the key of B-flat? Two flats.

NOTE TO TEACHER.—Further illustrations on this subject will not be necessary, since the principle is the same in each succeeding transposition.

16. Third transposition of the scale by fourths; from B♭ to E♭. A♭ is flat-seven to B♭. A♭, therefore, is the next flat introduced.

No. 63. Scale in Key of E-Flat. Ascending and descending.

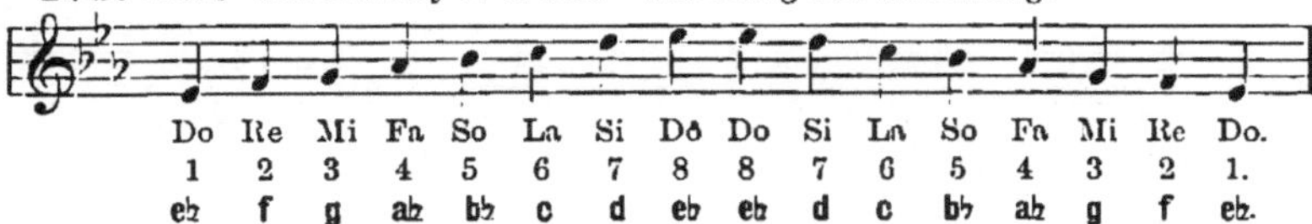
Do Re Mi Fa So La Si Do Do Si La So Fa Mi Re Do.
1 2 3 4 5 6 7 8 8 7 6 5 4 3 2 1.
e♭ f g a♭ b♭ c d e♭ e♭ d c b♭ a♭ g f e♭.

17. Fourth transposition of the scale by fourths; from E♭ to A♭. D♭ is flat-seven to E♭. D♭, therefore, is the next flat introduced.

No. 64. Scale in Key of A-Flat ascending. A descending form.

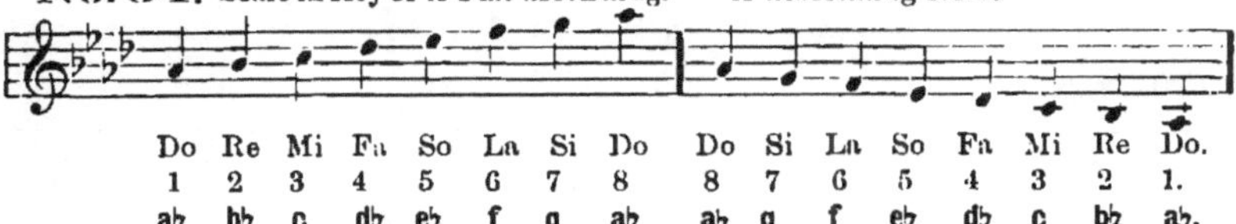
Do Re Mi Fa So La Si Do Do Si La So Fa Mi Re Do.
1 2 3 4 5 6 7 8 8 7 6 5 4 3 2 1.
a♭ b♭ c d♭ e♭ f g a♭ a♭ g f e♭ d♭ c b♭ a♭.

18. Fifth transposition by fourths; from A♭ to D♭. G♭ is therefore the next flat introduced.

19. Sixth transposition by fourths; from D♭ to G♭. C♭ is therefore the next flat introduced.

20. The scale may be still further transposed by fourths: to the Key of B♭♭, with nine flats (two double flats); to the key of E♭♭, with ten flats (three double flats); to the key of A♭♭, with eleven flats (four double flats); to the key of D♭♭, with twelve flats (five double flats); and so on.

NOTE 1.—The key of B♭♭ is the same to the ear as the key of C. The difference is not in the thing itself, but merely in the sign.

NOTE 2.—The keys beyond G♭ (six flats) are but seldom used, as the same variety may be more easily obtained in transposition by sharps. The keys beyond D♭ (five flats) are seldom used in church music.

No. 65. SINGING THROUGH ALL THE KEYS FOR DAILY PRACTICE.

Scale of C.
Arr. by T. E. P.
Do Re Mi Fa So La Si Do, The scale of C and prepare for
Scale of G.
G with its one sharp, Do Re Mi Fa So La Si Do, The scale of G now prepare for
Scale of D.
D with its two sharps, Do Re Mi Fa So La Si Do, The scale of D now prepare for
Scale of A.
A with its three sharps, Do Re Mi Fa So La Si Do, The scale of A now prepare for
Scale of E.
E with its four sharps, Do Re Mi Fa So La Si Do, The scale of E now prepare for
Scale of B.
B with its five sharps, Do Re Mi Fa So La Si Do, The scale of B now prepare for
Scale of F♯.
F sharp six sharps, Do Re Mi Fa So La Si Do, The scale of F sharp.

Enharmonic Change. Scale of G♭.
Now the Enhar - monic Change and sing the scale of G flat, Do Re Mi Fa So La Si
Scale of D♭.
Do, The scale of G flat prepare for D flat with five flats, Do Re Mi Fa So La Si
Scale of A♭.
Do, The scale of D flat prepare for A flat with four flats, Do Re Mi Fa So La Si
Scale of E♭.
Do, The scale of A flat prepare for E flat with three flats, Do Re Mi Fa So La Si
Scale of B♭.
Do The scale of E flat prepare for B flat with two flats, Do Re Mi Fa So La Si
Scale of F.
Do, The scale of B flat pre-pare for F with its one flat,
Scale of C.
Do Re Mi Fa So La Si Do, The scale of F and prepare for C the natural key,
C, the natural key. Where we began, now we end, you and me, Singing the scales from C to C.

PARAGRAPH XVIII.

MELODICS—*DIATONIC, MINOR AND MAJOR INTERVALS.

* Note.—Diatonic, because they are produced by the skips in the diatonic scale.

1. In addition to those intervals called steps and small steps, there are also other intervals occasioned by skipping; as Thirds, Fourths, Fifths, Sixths, Sevenths, and Octaves.

2. Intervals are always reckoned from the lowest tone upwards, unless otherwise expressed.

3. Two tones being the same pitch, are called UNISON, or said to be *in unison*.

4. The intervals between One and Two, or Two and Three, or between any tone and the tone that is represented on the degree of the staff, next above it, is called a *Second*.

NOTE.—Seconds are intervals of the same magnitude as steps and small steps.

5. *Seconds*—1st. A second consisting of a *small step*, is a MINOR (small) SECOND. 2nd. A second consisting of a *step*, is a MAJOR (great) SECOND.

6. The intervals between One and Three, or between Two and Four, or between any tone and the tone that is represented on the third degree of the staff, inclusive, is called a *Third*.

7. *Thirds*—1st. A third consisting of a *step* and a *small step*, is a MINOR THIRD. 2nd. A third consisting of *two steps*, is a MAJOR THIRD.

8. The interval between One and Four, or between Two and Five, is called a *Fourth*.

9. *Fourths*—1st. A fourth consisting of *two steps* and a *small step*, is a PERFECT FOURTH. 2nd. A fourth consisting of *three steps*, is a SHARP FOURTH.

10. The intervals between One and Five, or between Two and Six, is called a *Fifth*.

11. *Fifths*—1st. A fifth consisting of *two steps* and *two small steps*, is a FLAT (diminished) FIFTH. 2nd. A fifth consisting of *three steps* and a *small step*, is a PERFECT FIFTH.

12. The interval between One and Six, or between Two and Seven, is called a *Sixth*.

13. *Sixths*—1st. A sixth consisting of *three steps* and *two small steps*, is a MINOR SIXTH. 2nd. A sixth consisting of *four steps* and a *small step*, is a MAJOR SIXTH.

14. The intervals between One and Seven, or between Two and Eight, is called a *Seventh*.

15. *Sevenths*--1st. A seventh consisting of *four steps* and *two small steps*, is a FLAT (diminished) SEVENTH. 2nd. A seventh consisting of *five steps* and a *small step*, is a SHARP SEVENTH.

16. The intervals between One and Eight, or between Two and Nine (or *two* of the next series), is called an *Octave*.

17. *Octave*—An octave consists of *five steps* and *two small steps*.

NOTE.—In addition to the intervals already mentioned, there are others arising out of the chromatic scale, but as they rather belong to the study of harmony, further notice of them is omitted in this work

---

PARAGRAPH XIX.

CHROMATIC SCALE.

NOTE.—The Teacher may, with the aid of an instrument, teach the class to sing the Chromatic Scale. He can best do this by taking a part at a time. Thus, Teacher says, "Listen." Teacher plays and sings Do Di Re. Class sings it after him. Then Teacher sings Re Ri Mi. Class sings it. Then the Teacher, Do Di Re Ri Mi. Class sings it after him. In this way the Teacher may, in a short time, teach the class to sing the Chromatic scale, ascending and descending.

1. In addition to the scale already mentioned, called the Diatonic Scale, there is another scale formed by the introduction of the intermediate tones between those tones of the Diatonic Scale, which are separated by the interval of a step. The scale consists of thirteen tones, and twelve intervals of a half-step each; it is called the CHROMATIC SCALE.

2. The intermediate tones are named from either of the Diatonic Scale-tones between which they occur, with the addition of a sharp or flat prefixed or annexed. Thus, the intermediate tone between One and Two may be named Sharp-one, or Flat-two.

3. Characters called SHARPS and FLATS are used as signs of the intermediate tones, or of the tones named Sharp or Flat.

4. Sharps or Flats (signs) are canceled by a character called a NATURAL.

CHROMATIC SCALE—KEY OF C.
No. 66. With Absolute Names, Relative Names, and Syllables.
C, C-sharp, D, D-sharp, E, F, F-sharp, G, G-sharp, A, A-sharp, B, C,
1, sharp 1, 2, sharp 2, 3, 4, sharp 4, 5, sharp 5, 6, sharp 6, 7, 8,
Do, Di, Re, Ri, Mi, Fa, Fi, So, Si, La, Li, Si, Do,
C, B, B-flat, A, A-flat, G, G-flat, F, E, E-flat, D, D-flat, C,
8, 7, flat-7, 6, flat-6, 5, flat-5, 4, 3, flat-3, 2, flat-2, 1,
Do, Si, Se, La, Le, So, Se, Fa, Mi, Me, Re, Ra, Do,
No. 67. CHROMATIC SCALE—KEY OF D.
D, D-sharp, E, E-sharp, F-sharp, G, G-sharp, A, A-sharp, B, B-sharp, C-sharp, D,
1, sharp 1, 2, sharp 2, 3, 4, sharp 4, 5, sharp 5, 6, sharp 6, 7, 8,
Do, Di, Re, Ri, Mi, Fa, Fi, So, Si, La, Li, Si, Do,
D, C-sharp, C, B, B-flat, A, A-flat, G, F-sharp, F, E, E-flat, D.
8 7, flat 7, 6, flat 6, 5, flat 5, 4, 3, flat 3, 2, flat 2, 1.
Do, Si, Se, La, Le, So, Se, Fa, Mi, Me, Re, Ra, Do.
No. 68. Exercise with Sharp-four.
Do Re Mi Fa So Fi So So So Fi So La Si Do
See the ros - y morn-ing light, Smil-ing o'er the mead-ow bright;
Do Do Si So La Fi So Fi So La So La Si Do.
Up and quick-ly haste a - way— 'Tis a hap - py, hap - py day.
No. 69. Exercise introducing Flat-seven.
Do Si Do Se La La So La Si Do La Si Do Re
Sing-ing, sing - ing, wild and free, Sing-ing, sing - ing, glad are we;
Do Si Do La Se Se La So So La Si Do Re Do
Not a sor - row, not a care, On - ly pleas - ure now we share.

No. 70. Sharp-five and Flat-seven.

Do Si Do Si La Si La Si Do Re Si Do Do Do
O'er the burn - ing, thirst - y plain, Pours the wel - come, sum - mer rain;

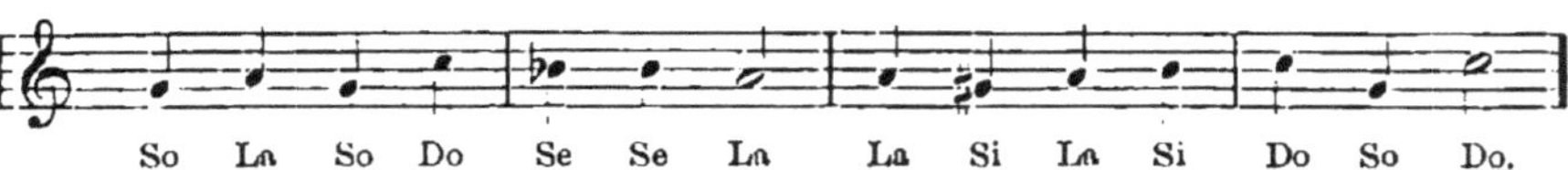
So La So Do Se Se La La Si La Si Do So Do.
'Tis the cool re - fresh - ing shower, Brighter makes each com - ing hour.

No. 71. Sharp-two. Three guides us to this tone.

Do Mi Ri Mi Fa So Mi So Re Do Mi Ri Mi Fa Mi Fa Re Do.
Life is like a fleet - ing day, O how soon it fades a - way.

No. 72. Sharp-four and Flat-six.

Do Mi So So Le So Fi So Do Do So La So Fi Fi So So Do.
Soft-ly, soft - ly, evening zephyrs blow, O'er the wa - ter mer-ri - ly we go.

No. 73. Sharp-one and Flat-three.

Do Re Me Do Re Di Re Me Fa So Fi So Me Re Di Re Me Do.
Here I wan - der dreari - ly a - lone, Ev - ery song-bird from the wood has flown.

No. 74. Sharp-six.

Do So Do Re Si Li Si Re Re Si So La Si Do.
Frown old win - ter if you will, We will all be hap - py still.

PARAGRAPH XX.

MELODICS—MINOR SCALE.

1. There is another Diatonic Scale, consisting also of eight tones, but differing in respect to its intervals, from the one already explained, and is called the MINOR SCALE. The former scale is called the MAJOR SCALE.

2. The following forms of the Minor Scale are now in use:

1st. The *Natural Minor Scale*, consists of the following tones: A, B, C, D, E, F, G, A.

No. 75.

La Si Do Re Mi Fa So La

The intervals are as follows: from One to Two, a step; from Two to Three, a small step; from Three to Four, a step: from Four to Five, a step; from Five to Six, a small step; from Six to Seven, a step; from Seven to Eight, a step.

2nd. The *Harmonic or Regular Minor Scale*, consists of the following tones: A, B, C, D, E, F, G♯, A, and differs from the natural form by the introduction of *Sharp-seven.*

No. 76.

La Si Do Re Mi Fa Si La

The intervals are as follows: between One and Two, a step: between Two and Three, a small step; between Three and Four, a step; between Four and Five, a step; between Five and Six, a small step; between Six and Seven, a step and a small step; and between Seven and Eight, a small step.

3rd. The *Melodic or Irregular Minor Scale.* In this form the Sharp-six and Sharp-seven are both used in the ascending series. It is only Minor in lower tones, the upper part of the Scale being Major. In connection with this form of the ascending Minor Scale, it is common to use the natural form in descending. It consists of the tones A, B, C, D, E, F♯, G♯, A.

No. 77. Ascending. Descending.

La Si Do Re Mi Fi Si La
La So Fa Mi Re Do Si La.

The intervals are as follows: from One to Two, a step; from Two to Three, a small step; from Three to Four, a step; from Four to Five, a step; from Five to Six, a step; from Six to Seven, a step; and from Seven to Eight, a small step.

3. The Minor scale, in its natural position, commences with A, or A is taken as One, in the above examples.

4. When the Major and Minor Scales have the same signature, they are said to be related. So every Major Scale has its relative Minor, and every Minor Scale has its relative Major.

5. The relative Minor to any Major Scale is based upon its sixth, and the relative Major to any Minor Scale is based upon its third.

6. The letters and syllables correspond in the Major and its relative Minor. Thus Do is applied to C in both cases, although it is One in the Major, and Three in the Minor Scale, etc.

Question.—What other Diatonic Scale is there besides the Major? In what respect does the Minor Scale differ from the Major? Ans. In the order of the intervals. How many forms of the Minor Scale are there in common use? When are the Major and Minor Scale said to be related? How much higher is the Major Scale than the relative Minor? How much lower is the Minor Scale than its relative Major? What is the relative Minor to C Major? What is the relative Major to A Minor? etc. In C Major, what tone of the scale is C? In A Minor, what tone is C? In A Minor, what tone of the scale is A? In C Major, what tone of the Scale is A? What is the signature of C Major? To A Minor? etc.

Note—The distinguishing feature of the Major and Minor Scale is the third. The Major Scale is known by its Major third, and the Minor scale is known by its Minor third.

MAJOR SCALES, WITH THEIR RELATIVE MINORS.

No. 78. Scale of C Major. (No Signature).
Do Re Mi Fa So La Si Do Do Si La So Fa Mi Re Do.
No. 79. Scale of A Minor. (No Signature).
La Si Do Re Mi Fa Si La La Si Fa Mi Re Do Si La.
No. 80. Scale of G Major. (One Sharp).
No. 81. Scale of E Minor. (One Sharp).
No. 82. Scale of D Major. (Two Sharps).
No. 83. Scale of B Minor. (Two Sharps).
No. 84. Scale of A Major. (Three Sharps).
No. 85. Scale of F-Sharp Minor. (Three Sharps).
No. 86. Scale of E Major. (Four Sharps).
No. 87. Scale of C-Sharp Minor. (Four Sharps).

No. 88. Scale of B Major. (Five Sharps).
No. 89. Scale of G-Sharp Minor. (Five Sharps).
No. 90. Scale of F Major. (One Flat).
No. 91. Scale of D Minor. (One Flat).
No. 92. Scale of B-Flat Major. (Two Flats).
No. 93. Scale of G Minor. (Two Flats).

PARAGRAPH XXI.

DYNAMICS—DEGREES—FORM OF DELIVERY OF TONE.

1. A medium tone, produced by the ordinary exertion of the vocal organs, is called MEZZO (pronounced Mate-zo) and marked *mez.* or *m.*

2. A soft tone, produced by less than ordinary exertion of the vocal organs, is called PIANO (pronounced *pee-an-o*) and marked *p.*

3. A loud tone, produced by a strong or full exertion of the vocal organs, is called FORTE (pronounced *for-ta*), and marked *for.* or *f.*

4. A tone, produced by a very small but careful exertion of the vocal organs, softer than Piano, yet loud enough to be a good audible sound, is called PIANISSIMO (pronounced *pee-an-is-si-mo*), and marked *pp.*

5. A tone, produced with a greater exertion of the vocal organs than is required for Forte, but not so loud as to degenerate into a scream, is called FORTISSIMO, and marked *ff.*

NOTE—Mezzo, Piano, and Forte are Italian words, which, by long usage, have become technical terms in music, and are used by all nations.

QUESTIONS. What is the third distinction in musical sounds? What is the department called, which rises out of this distinction? What is the subject of Dynamics? When a tone is neither loud nor soft, what is it called? How marked? When a tone is soft, what is it called? How marked? When a tone is loud, what is it called? How marked? If a tone is very soft what is it called? How marked? If a tone is very loud, what is it called? How marked? What does Piano, or *p*. signify? What does Forte, or *f*, signify? What does Mezzo, or *m*, signify? What does Pianissimo, or *pp*, signify? What does Fortissimo, or *ff*, signify?

There are six principal forms of tones, as follows :

6. A tone begun, continued, and ended, with an equal degree of force, is called the ORGAN TONE, indicated thus, ═════.

7. A tone beginning soft and gradually increasing to loud, is called the CRESCENDO, indicated thus, <.

8. A tone beginning loud and gradually diminishing to soft, is called the DIMINUENDO, indicated thus, >.

9. The union of the Crescendo and the Dimuendo, is called the SWELL, indicated thus, <>.

10. A very sudden Crescendo, is called the PRESSURE TONE, indicated thus, <.

11. A tone very suddenly diminished, is called an EXPLOSIVE TONE, or SFORZANDO, indicated thus, >.

QUESTIONS.—When a tone is begun, continued, and ended, with an equal degree of power, what is it called? When a tone is begun soft and gradually increased to loud, what is it called? When a tone is begun loud, and diminished to soft, what is it called? When the Crescendo is united to the Diminuendo, what is it called? What is a very sudden Crescendo called? What is a very sudden Diminuendo called?

12. When a passage is performed in a close, smooth, gliding manner, it is said to be LEGATO (⁀).

13. When a passage is performed in a pointed, distinct, and articulate manner, it is said to be STACCATO (' ' ' ').

14. A less degree of Staccato is called MARCATO, and is marked thus, (. . . .).

15. A character, called a TIE, is used to show how many notes are to be sung to one syllable. It is also used to denote the LEGATO style (⁀).

16. When a note or rest is to be prolonged beyond its usual time, a character, called a PAUSE, is placed over or under it (𝄐).

17. A BRACE is used to connect the Staves on which the different parts are written ( ).

18. The DIRECT (𝆙) is sometimes used at the end of a Staff, to show on what degree of the following Staff the first note is placed.

PARAGRAPH XXII.

DYNAMICS—EXPRESSION OF WORDS AND MISCELLANEOUS DIRECTIONS.

1. The vowel sounds only should be prolonged in singing. The voice dwells on these alone, so they should be delivered with accuracy, and carefully sustained, without being changed. The organs of sound should be kept in one position, while sustaining the sound, and no change should be allowed with the lips, teeth, tongue or throat, or even the body until the sound is finished.

NOTE—It is a very common fault for singers to change the tonic sounds, and dwell not on the *radical*, but on the vanish or closing sound; thus *a* becomes *e*, and *o* becomes *oo*, &c. In the word great, for example, instead of dwelling steadily upon the vowel sound *a*, the singer changes it to *e*,, and that which should be grea - t, becomes grea - e - t so also in the syllable applied to Two; let it be Ra instead of Ra - e - -

2. A distinct articulation is entirely dependent upon the manner in which the consonants are delivered. These should be produced in a quick, smart manner, and with great precision. Neglect in this respect is the great cause of indistinctness in singing.

3. Accent to music is what emphasis is to reading or speaking. In accent we are governed by two laws, the one strictly mechanical, the other based upon common sense. The mechanical accent in a two part measure, is a regularly recurring stress, upon the first part of the measure. In a three part measure, upon the first part of the measure. In a four part measure, there are two accents, one on the first part of the measure, and the other on the third part of the measure, the first accent being almost twice as strong as the second. The word *heavy* is used in describing the first accent, the word *light* describing the second. The words *primary* and *secondary* are also used in this connection.

In the six part measure the *heavy* accent occurs on the first part of the measure, the *light* on the fourth part of the measure. The mechanical law should be taught as thoroughly by the teacher as the beating of time or the marking the parts of the measure by motions of the hand. The common-sense law should be taught when the words and music are combined, and *then,* those words and syllables of words, which are *more* or *less* emphatic in reading or speaking, should receive a *greater* or *less* accent in singing.

4. Pauses, both *grammatical* and *rhetorical,* are also essential to good singing. When necessary, they must be obtained by shortening the preceding note, as in the following example:

No. 94.

Written.
Sung.
Hark, hark the sound of joy and mirth.
Hark, hark the sound of joy and mirth.

5. Emphasis. Emphatic words should be given with greater or less power (often with *sf.*) without reference to rhythmic accent. In common psalmody its application is difficult, from the frequent want of a proper adaptation of the poetry to the music. The effect of emphasis may often be increased by a momentary pause (see 4).

6. The mouth should, in general, be freely opened. It is very common for singers not to open their mouths sufficiently wide as to give a free and full passage to the sound.

7. Directions in regard to taking Breath.

1. In taking breath, make as little noise as possible.
2. Let it be done quickly, and *without any change in the position of the mouth.*
3. Never breathe between the different syllables of the same word.
4. When several notes come together to one syllable, do not breathe between them, except in long running passages, where it cannot be avoided.
5. Words intimately connected, as the article and its noun, the preposition and its noun, should not be separated by taking breath.
6. The practice of always breathing at a particular part of the measure, should be avoided.
7. Take breath only when necessary.

8. Quality of Tone.—The essential qualities of a good tone are purity, fullness, firmness and certainty.

1. A tone is Pure when free from all hissing and huskiness.
2. A tone is Full when it is delivered by a free and natural use of the vocal organs.

3 and 4. A tone is *firm* and *certain* which, when correctly given, is held without change and perfectly controlled by the performer.

The following are faults, viz:

1. Striking below the proper sound and sliding up to it, as from Five to Eight, etc.

2. A wavering or trembling of the voice.

3. A change just at the close of a tone, produced by a careless relaxation of the organs, which should always be held firm in the proper position, until the sound ceases.

4. To Correct Faults. —When the teacher discovers a fault, it is not enough to say that a fault exists, but the teacher must show it by his own performance, until the pupil has a clear idea of it, and knows how to avoid it.

5. In singing, try to enter into the spirit of the words. Avoid a heavy, unfeeling, machine-like style of performance, cultivating that which comes from the heart, having some character and soul in it, and appropriate to both words and music. The composer furnishes the inanimate form, and it depends upon the performer whether that form shall live, and take hold of the affections and feelings of others—producing the effects for which music was designed.

PARAGRAPH XXIII.

PRONUNCIATION AND ARTICULATION.

Pronunciation in singing is subjected to the same rule as in speech. Good pronunciation consists in giving to each syllable the sound which belongs to it; but as syllables have generally greater force and duration when sung, and as defects become thus more striking, more care is necessary, to follow the directions given in grammar, for the formation of each syllable. The rolling of the R. or the hissing of the S, must be avoided; but it is very necessary that the vowels should receive their proper sounds.

We would advise pupils to articulate rather extravagantly in study; for then, if in singing before people they lose a little of their precision, they will still have enough to do well.

Pronunciation of The, By, My, &c.

The, before a word beginning with a vowel, should have nearly the long sound of *e*, as in *relate;* before a word beginning with a *consonant*, the obscure sound as in *her*, but never the sound of broad *a*. The *y* in *By* should generally be full.

My should always be pronounced with the short sound of *i*, mentioned above, unless, in emphatic expression, or in solemn style; and, in the latter, only in phrases directly associated with solemnity, as in the following; "my God." The word *myself* should never have the long *y*.

The termination *ed* should be pronounced as a separate syllable, in *chanting*. In singing, it should be pronounced or omitted as the meter demands.

In the words *Guide, Guard, Regard, Sky, Kind,* &c., we must follow general custom as it is the only law of spoken language. In cultivated usage they are pronounced with a slight sound of *y* following *g* and *k*.

The word Amen.

Vocal music of a sacred character, is properly allowed the same liberty which is conceded in the language of poetry, with regard to the use of style of pronunciation which is obsolete, for common purposes, but appropriate in the expression of deep, solemn, grand, or lofty effects of emotion. Hence the just preference, in the singing of sacred music, for the pronunciation of the word *Amen*, with *a* broad, as in *arm:* thus, *ah-men.*

PARAGRAPH XXIV.

THE VOICE—RESPIRATION—HINTS TO TEACHERS.

THE VOICE.

The voice is the most beautiful of all instruments, and at the same time the most delicate. In order to preserve it, excesses of all kinds must be avoided. The cultivation of the vocal organs or muscles is physiologically similar to the cultivation of the muscles of the arm. Daily practice is necessary, but always leave off before you are fatigued.

With time, patience, and the direction of a teacher who has the *true system of voice-training,* persons with voices below mediocre may become excellent singers. There is truly but one method, and but few who really understand how to teach it.

RESPIRATION.

In singing, a tone is breath vocalized; how important, then, that the teacher and pupil should pay great attention to the subject of Respiration. The use of the voice depends very largely upon respiratory action. From long experience the writer has found that a combined action of the diaphragm with the abdominal muscles is the most practical, healthful and beneficial. The Respiratory action should be removed as far as possible from the throat. The diaphragm is the great respirating muscle and forms the floor (so to speak) of the lungs and the ceiling of the stomach. Combine its action with the abdominal muscles, and you have the most perfect and healthful manner of respiration; in order to sing well, one must be *well* physically, hence the necessity of cultivating such habits of respiration as will conduce to a healthy state of the vocal organs. The voice is produced by the air coming in contact (in its passage from the lungs through the trachea or windpipe) with muscles called the vocal chords which are situated in the larynx, (known as Adam's Apple). This vocalized air is then received into the Pharynx (the back part of the throat) which is the principal modifier of the tone. The soft-palate, mouth, lips, tongue, teeth, etc., also assist in the modification of the tone. The natural quality of the voice is generally intense and clear. Use as little breath as possible. Avoid all muscular exertion in the throat. Remember that the diaphragm with the abdominal muscles should perform the principal part of the labor.

HINTS TO THE TEACHER.

The order in which the different topics are presented is not imperative, as one topic cannot be finished without introducing some other. The teacher cannot proceed far in the subject of Melodics with profit to the pupil unless the subject of Rhythmics is introduced, and it is equally certain that neither pitch or time lessons can be judiciously taught without attention being given to the use of the voice and a correct style of singing. The teacher in his first lesson may give a short analysis of sound. Sound is a sensation resulting from certain vibrations or sound waves in the atmosphere; these sound waves being generated by some vibrating or moving body: as any substance thrown in the smooth water, at one point, sends waves as the result across its surface. Sounds are classified as Musical and Noise.

The sound waves in noise are confused and irregular, in musical sounds they are symmetrical and follow each other at uniform distance. The pitch of musical sounds depends on the length of the sound wave. Long waves produce *low* tones, short waves *high* tones; these results are attained by the slowness or quickness of motion of the vibrating body.

The peculiar quality of sound produced by any instrument or voice is called its *timbre.*

Sound waves of the same length may differ in their intensity or force, hence the different degrees of loudness in sounds.

Melody is a succession of single sounds—In Harmony several sounds are heard at once—for instance the *Triad*, 1, 3, 5.

The starting point of the scale series, is known as the *Tonic* or *Key-note.* Two in the scale is called (in Harmony) technically the *Super-Tonic.* Three the *Mediant.* Four the *Sub-Dominant.* Five is called the *Dominant.* Six the *Sub-Mediant.* Seven the *Leading-Note* or *Sub-Tonic.* Eight also bears the name of *Tonic.* The term Tonic or Key-note is frequently used, the other terms rarely so.

We cannot refrain from urging the teacher to remember the necessity for constant scale practice, in the development of the sense of tune.

The absolute pitch of sounds is determined by the actual number of vibrations in a second of time. For instance a sound whose vibrations are 254 in a second, is found to be in the upper part of the male voice, and in the lower part of the female voice. This is found in the middle of the piano-forte key-board, and is called the "middle C." The octave below middle C having 132 vibrations per second, is written small C. The next octave, 66 vibrations, is sung only by men having exceptionally low voices. The octave above the middle C has 528 vibrations. The next octave above, 1056 vibrations, and is only reached by women and sometimes boys having remarkably high voices. The middle C being reached by all voices occupies a position between the two staves, its line being the first added line above the lower staff, and the first added line below the upper staff.

A dot placed after a note or rest increases the value of the note one half of its former value. The second dot adds half as much as the first. Thus a double-dotted quarter note, is equal to seven sixteenths.

In commencing an exercise the pitch or key-note should be distinctly given by the teacher, and where the exercise commences with some other sound than the key-note, *that sound* should be traced from the key-note, and then distinctly sung as the starting note, before commencing the exercise.

EXPLANATION OF MUSICAL TERMS.

A—an Italian preposition, meaning, in, for, at, with, &c.
Accelerando—increasing the time faster and yet more fast.
Adagio, or *Adasio*—slow.
Adagio Assai, or *Molto*—more slow, or very slow.
Ad Libitum—at pleasure, especially regarding time.
Affettuoso—tender and affecting.
Agitato—in an agitated manner.
Alla Capella—in Church style.
Allegro—fast.
Allegro Assai—faster.
Allegretto—not so fast as Allegro.
Allegro ma non Troppo—fast, but not too fast.
Amabile—in an amiable manner, affectionately.
Amateur—one who practices music for pleasure.
Amoroso, or *Con Amore*—in a soft, delicate, amatory style.
Andante—tender, distinct, and rather slow, yet connected.
Andante Con Moto—movement quicker than Andante.
Andantino—somewhat faster than Andante.
Animato, or *Con Anima*—with spirit, courage, and boldness.
Antiphone—music sung by alternate choirs.
Ardito—bold and energetic.
Arioso—in a light, airy, singing manner.
A Tempo—to return to original time.
A Tempo Giusto—in strict time.
Ben Marcato—in appointed and well-marked manner.
Bis—twice,—a call for a repetition of a performance.
Brillante—brilliant, gay, shining, sparkling.
Cadence—closing strain; also a fanciful, extemporaneous embellishment at the close of a song.
Cadenza—same as the second use of Cadence. See Cadence.
Calando—softer and slower.
Cantabile—graceful, singing style; a pleasing, flowing melody.
Canto—the treble part in a chorus.
Choir—a company or band of singers; also that part of a church appropriated to the singers.
Chorister—a member of a choir of singers.
Col, or *Con*—with.
Con Spirito—with spirit.
Comodo, or *Commodo*—in an easy and unrestrained manner.
Con Affetto—smooth, tender, affecting style.
Con Dolcessa—with delicacy.
Con Dolore, or *Con Duolo*—see *Doloroso*.
Conductor—one who superintends a musical performance; same as Music Director.
Con Energico—with energy.
Con Espressione—with expression.
Con Fuoco—with ardor, fire.
Con Grazia—with grace and elegance.
Con Impeto—with impetuosity.
Con Moto—with commotion.
Con Spirito—with spirit, animation.
Da—for, by, of, from.
Da Capo al Fine—from the beginning to the end.
Da Capo al Segno—repeat from the sign.
Declamando—in the style of declamation.
Decrescendo—diminishing, decreasing.
Devozione—devotional, devoutly.
Dilettante—a lover of the arts in general, or a lover of music.
Dolce—soft, smooth and delicate.
Dolente—mournful.
Doloroso—in a soft and pathetic style.
E—and.
Elegante—Elegance.
Encore—more, (give us more).
Energico, or *Con Energia*—with energy.
Espressivo—with expression.
Fine, *Fin*, or *Finale*—the end.
Forzando, *Forz.*, or *fz*—sudden increase of power <.
Fugue—a composition which repeats or sustains, in its several parts throughout, the subject with which it commences, and which is often led off by some one of its parts.
Fugato—in the fugue style.
Fughetta—A little fugue.
Grazioso—smoothly, gracefully.
Grave—a very slow, grave and solemn movement.
Impressario—a manager or conductor of concerts and operas.
Lachrimoso—mournful, tearful.
Lamentevole, Lamentando, Lamentabile—mournfully.
Largo—slow.
Larghetto—slow, but not so slow as Largo.
Larghissimo—extremely slow.
Legato—close, smooth and gliding manner.
Lento, or *Lentamente*—slow.
Lentando—gradually slower and softer.
Ma—but.
Maestoso—with dignity and majesty.
Maestro Di Capella—chapel master, or conductor of church music.
Marcato—in strong and marked style.
Moderato—moderately, in moderate time.
Molto—much or very.
Molto Voce—with a very full voice.
Mordente—a trill or shake.
Morendo—gradually dying away.
Mosso—motion.
Moto—with movement.
Non Troppo—not too fast.
Orchestra—a company or band of instrumental performers; also that part of a theatre occupied by the band.
Pastorale—applied to soft rural movements generally written in 12-8 time.
Piano, Pia.—soft.
Piu—more.
Piu Mosso—with more motion, faster.
Pizzicato—snapping the violin string with the fingers.
Poco—a little.
Poco Adagio—a little slow.
Poco a Poco—little by little, gradually.
Portamento—the manner of carrying the voice from one tone to another.
Precentor—conductor, leader of a congregation.
Presto—fast.
Prestissimo—very fast.
Rallentando—slower and softer by degrees.
Recitando—a speaking manner of performance, in the style of recitative.
Recitative—musical recitation.
Rinforzando, Rinf., Rinforzo—suddenly increasing in power
Ritardando—slower and slower by degrees.
Semplice—chaste, simple.
Sempre—throughout, always; as, *Sempre Forte*—loud throughout.
Senza—without; as *Senza Organo*—without the organ.
Sforzando, Sforzato—with strong force of emphasis, rapidly diminishing.
Siciliana—a movement of light, graceful character in 6 or 12-8 time.
Smorendo, Smorzando—to gradually diminish in Legato manner. (See Morendo).
Soave, Soavemento—sweet, sweetly. See Dolce.
Solfeggio—a vocal exercise for sol-fa-ing.
Solo—For a single voice or instrument.
Sostenuto—sustaining tones to their full length.
Sotto—under, below. *Sotto Voce*—with subdued voice.
Spirito—spirit.
Staccato—short, detached, distinct.
Subito—quick.
Tace, or *Tacet*—silent, or be silent.
Tardo—slow.
Tasto Solo—without chords.
Tempo—time. *Tempo a Piacere*—time at pleasure.
Ten, *Tenuto*—hold on. See Sostenuto.
Tutti—the whole, full chorus or orchestra.
Un—a; as *Un Poco*—a little.
Va—go on; as *Va Crescendo*—continue to increase.
Verse—same as Solo.
Vigoroso—bold, energetic.
Vivace—quick and cheerful.
Virtuoso—a proficient in art.
Voce di Petto—the chest voice.
Voce di Testa—the head voice.
Voce Sola—voice alone, without accompaniment.
Volti Subito—turn over quickly.

See, the Morn is Breaking.

FANNY J. CROSBY.
THEODORE E. PERKINS.
1. See, the morn is breaking, Ten - der blossoms wak - ing, Leaf - y beds for - sak - ing,
2. See, the morn is breaking, Now the birds a - wak - ing, Drops of dew are shaking,
3. Morn thy hours are fleetest, But thy joys are sweetest, Cheer-i - ly thou greetest,
Hail the light so dear; Now with grateful feel - ing, Distant sounds are steal - ing,
From their crested wings; What a sky hangs o'er us, What a scene be - fore us,
Ev - ery wea - ry heart; While thy cheek is glowing, Ros - y health be - stow - ing,
Life a - new re - veal - ing To the list - 'ning ear. Hail! in thy beauty,
While her tune - ful cho - rus, Joy - ful na - ture sings.
In thy pleas - ure flow - ing, All may share a part.
Gen - tle blush - ing morn: We come to greet thee, Love - ly smil - ing morn.

I Am a Lily.

GRACE J. FRANCES.
HUBERT P. MAIN.
1. I am a lil - y, I bloom in a vale, I smile to the morning and
2. I am a lil - y, how blest is my lot, I cheer with my fragrance a
3. I am a lil - y, and if you would see How happy the children of
4. I am a lil - y, tho' brief is my day, In pleasure and sunshine 'tis
sigh in the gale; I toil not to pur - chase the rai - ment I wear, Yet
pal - ace and cot, I view not with en - vy the rose in her pride, But
na - ture can be; Then come to our dwelling so love - ly and fair, We'll
fad - ing a - way; When summer no long - er trips o - ver the lawn, With
monarchs might envy its beau - ty so rare.
dwell in con - tentment and joy by her side.
greet you with mu - sic and welcome you there.
all her young blossoms, I too, shall be gone.
CHORUS
I am a lil - y, I bloom in a vale, I smile to the morning and sigh to the gale; I love my companions my sweet sis - ter flowers, And share with them glad - ly the dew - drops and showers.

Hark, the Summer Birds.

Fanny J. Crosby.
Arr. Theodore E. Perkins.
1. Hark! the summer birds are call - ing, Hear their wild and mer-ry lay; Come where
2. Still a - gain those minstrel voic - es Long and loud their songs re - peat, While the
3. Come and join the woodland chor-us; Come and see the sparkling rills, On with
all with joy is glowing, To the woods a - way, a - way; Neath the tall and state-ly
playful winds in - vite us To their cool and calm re - treat; Nature like a gen - tle
ev - er rest-less murmur, Flowing down the verdant hills; Come and join the wood-land
branches Waving in the gol-den light, Where the sweetest flow'rs are blooming, Let us
moth - er, Smiles her opening buds to see There a - mid the blushing ros - es, O how
chor - us, Bid the slumbering echoes wake; While the bu-gles distant mu - sic Floats a -
La la la la la la la la la la la la la
sing from morn till night. La la la la la la la la la la la la la la
hap - py we shall be.
long the sil - ver lake.
la la la la la la la la la la la la la la la la la.
la la la la la la la la la la la la la la la la la.

I Love to Sing.

Geo W. Bethune, D. D.
Wm. B. Bradbury, by per.
Moderato.
1. I love to sing when I am glad, Song is the ech - o of my
2. Whene'er I greet the morning light, Sweet mu- sic flows in thankful
gladness; I love to sing when I am sad, Till song makes sweet my ver - y
numbers, And, 'mid the shadows of the night, I sing me to my welcome
sad - ness, Till song makes sweet my ver - y sad - ness, La la la la la
slum- bers, I sing me to my wel - come slum- bers, La la la la la
la, la la la la la la. la la la la la la la la la la la.
la la la, la la la, la, la, la, la.
Cres.
'Tis pleasant time when voices chime To some sweet rhyme in concert on - ly,
My heart is stirred by each glad bird, Whose notes are heard in summer bowers;

I Love to Sing. Concluded.
And song to me is compa - ny, Good compa-ny when I am lone-ly.
And song gives birth to friendly mirth, Around the hearth in wintry hours.
Night! Lovely Night!
T. F. Seward.
Arr. from Mendelssohn.
Con Spirito.
1. Night, love - ly night! I sing thy won - drous beau - ty;
Per - fumes, so rare, From blos - soms sweet as - cend - ing,
2. Bright - ly the moon O'er hill and val - ley shin - ing,
Soon, ah! too soon Her pearl - y rays de - clin - ing,
Stars shin - ing bright O - ver field and flower;
Fill all the air, Like a fra - grant bower.
Robes ev - ery tree With its sil - very light;
Leave in its dark - ness The si - lent night.
Fine.
No glare of day can e - qual thee, Thou dark and si - lent mys - ter - y;
What mar - vels are be - neath thee hid, O thou mys - ter - ious night!
D. C.

Snow is Falling.

MAYDEW.
THEODORE E. PERKINS.
1. Snow is falling— voices calling—Hark! the merry shout! Bells are ringing-maidens singing-
2. Snow is gleaming faces beaming As we glide along; Sleigh-bells jingling-glad hearts mingling
All the town are out. Oh, the laughing and the chatting, Glowing with de-light;
In our sleighing song. Oh, the ringing and the singing, All the earth is bright;
CHORUS.
Moonlight streaming—bright eyes beaming—What a joy-ous sight! Twinkling soft the
Young hearts quiver like a riv-er In the clear moon-light.
sleigh-bells sing With a glad and mer-ry ring; Oh, the snow, the joy-ous snow,
Boys and girls are all aglow; Listen to our happy song, While we swiftly glide along.

Where the Warbling Waters Flow.

Grazioso.
DUET.
Brinley Richards.
Where the warb - ling waters flow, And the Zeph - yrs gent - ly blow, Where the
Where the warb - ling waters flow, And the Zeph - yrs gent - ly blow, Where tho
warb - ling waters flow, And the Zephyrs gent-ly blow, The Fairies
warb - ling waters flow, And the Zephyrs gent-ly blow, The Fairies dwell, The Fairies
dwell, In grassy dell, Where the for - est flowers grow— And the
dwell, In grassy dell, In grassy dell, Where the for - est flowers grow— And the
ff Rit. pp a tempo.
ff rall. pp

ff Rit. pp a tempo.
Zephyrs gent-ly blow, Where the for - est flowers grow, And the Zephyrs gently
Zephyrs gent-ly blow, Where the for - est flowers grow, And the Zephyrs gently
ff Rall. pp
Rall.
Vivace.
blow, And a joyous home is theirs, For it knows not mortal cares;
Piu lento.
And its
Tempo primo.
ff p
And its
on-ly tear, Is the dew-drop clear; That the bend - ing li - ly bears—And its
ff p
a tempo.

ff
on - ly tear, Is the dew-drop clear; That the bend - ing li - ly bears, And the
on - ly tear, Is the dew-drop clear; That the bend - ing li - ly bears, And the
Rall. Dim.
ff
a tempo.
f
on - ly tear, Is the dew-drop clear; That the bend - ing li - ly bears, That the
on - ly tear, Is the dew-drop clear; That the bend - ing li - ly bears, That the
p
Cres.
f
bend - ing li - ly bears, That the bend - ing li - ly bears.
bend - ing li - ly bears, That the bend - ing li - ly bears.
Rall.

Hail to the Queen of Night.

GERMAN.

Maestoso.
1. Hail to the Queen of the silent night, Shine clear, shine bright, Yield thy pensive light;
2. Dart thy pure beams from thy throne on high, Beam on, thro' sky, Rob'd in a-zure dye;
Blith - ly we'll dance in thy sil - ver ray, Hap - pi - ly pass-ing the hours a - way.
We'll laugh and we'll sport while the night-bird sings, Flapping the dew from his sable wings:
Must we not love the stil - ly night, Dress'd in her robes of blue and white?
Sprites love to sport in the still moon-light, Play with the pearls of shadowy night;
Heaven's arch - es ring, Stars wink and sing, Hail, si - lent night!
Then let us sing, Time's on the wing, Hail, si - lent night!
Fai - ry moonlight, fairy moonlight, fairy moon - - - light.
fairy, fairy, fairy moon-light.

Alpine Song.

FANNY J VAN ALSTYNE.
HUBERT P. MAIN, by per.
1. Hur - rah! wel - come the day, Tra la la la la la la! A - way, let us a - way, Tra la la la la la la! We'll
2. Hur - rah! mer - ry are we, Tra la la la la la la! The stag you - der we see, Tra la la la la la la! Then
3. A - way, hun - ters, a - way! Tra la la la la la la! We'll soon cap - ture the prey, Tra la la la la la la! Then
climb to yon - der rock - y steep, Our Al - pine song re - peating, While far and clear the bu - gle's note With joy our ear shall greet.
gai - ly on, while spear and lance In morning's light are gleaming; No fainting heart, nor flagging steed, Till ro - sy eve shall beam.
gathered safe with friends at home, Our Al - pine song re - peating, The gen - tle tones we dear - ly love With joy our ear shall greet.
CHORUS.
Hur - rah! welcome the day, Tra la la la la la la la! A - way! a - way! A - way to the hills, a - way!

Like the Lark.

DUET.

FRANZ ABT.

Allegretto.
Lively.
1. Like the Lark would I were sing - ing Thro' the
2. Like the Lark would I were drink - ing Draughts of
mf
a - zure plains on high, O - ver hill and val - ley bring - ing, O - ver
pur - est morn - ing air, Till on dew - y flow - rets sink - ing. Till on
1st VOICE.
2d VOICE.
BOTH.
hill and val - ley bringing Dreams of spring along the sky, Dreams of spring along the
dew - y flow - rets sink - ing I could bask in fragrance rare, I could bask in fragrance
p
1st VOICE.
2d VOICE.
sky, O - ver hill and val - ley bring - ing, O - ver hill and val - ley
rare, Till on dew - y flow - 'rets sink - ing, Till on dew - y flow - 'rets

BOTH.
bringing, Dreams of spring a - long the sky, Dreams of spring a - long the sky.
sink - ing, I could bask in fragrance rare, I could bask in fragr ance rare.

The Song of the Bee.

REV. ALFRED TAYLOR, by per.

Buz - z, This is the song of the bee: His legs are of yel - low, A jol - ly good

fel - low, And yet a great worker is he. FINE.

1. { In days that are sun - ny He's getting his hon - ey; In days that are cloud-y He's mak - ing his wax:
   On pinks and on lil - ies, And gay daf - fo - dil - lies, And col - umbine blossoms, He le - vies a tax! }

2. { The sweet smelling clo - ver, He humming, hangs o - ver; The scent of the ros - es Makes fragrant his wings:
   He nev - er gets la - zy From this - tle or dai - sy, And weeds of the meadow, Some treasure he brings. }

3. { From morning's first gray light, Till fad - ing of daylight, He's sing - ing and toil - ing The summer day through:
   Oh! we may get wea - ry, And think work is drea - ry: 'Tis hard - er by far, to Have noth - ing to do! }

D. C. CHORUS.

Cheerily, Lightly Row.

Grace J. Frances.
Hubert P. Main.
1. Cheer-i - ly, cheer - i - ly, lightly row, While o - ver the bil - low so free, The
2. Stead-i - ly on-ward our course we keep, As gay as the bird on its wing; The
bark we are guid-ing is grace-ful - ly glid-ing, Ah, who are so hap - py as
plash of the oar, and the murmur of wa - ters, Keep time to the mu - sic we
we? The moonbeams are dancing a - long the waves, That murmur soft as they
sing. We wel - come the beau-ti - ful star - ry night, When balmy winds gently
flow. And bright are the glances from eyes that we love, As o - ver the sparkling
blow, And bright are the glances, &c.
deep we row, As mer - ri - ly, cheer - i - ly on we row, we row.

The Song of the Cobbler.

C. M. WARD. THEODORE E. PERKINS.

1. Wand'ring up and down one day, I peeped in the win - dow
2. See, how neat - ly o'er the last He draws down the leath - er,
3. Now with ham - mer hear him tap The shoe now so firm - ly
4. With his awl he makes a hole, First in - to the up - per,
5. Now with ham - mer, now with stitch, For this is the cob - bler's
o - ver the way, And, put - ting his need - dle through and through,
mak - ing it fast, And, put - ting his "waxed ends" through and through,
fixed in his lap, And, mov - ing his head both up and down,
then through the sole, Then, put - ing his pegs in, one or two,
way to get rich; He whis - tles and sings, that cob - bler, still,
CHORUS.
There sat a cob - bler mak - ing a shoe. Rat - a - tap, tap,
Ev - er his hands and bod - y works, too.
Yet on his face there's nev - er a frown.
Laugh - ing a - way, he hammers them through.
Do - ing his work with mer - ry good will.
Tick - a - tack, too, This is the way I make a shoe;
Rat - a - tap, tap, Tick - a - tack, too, This is the way I make a shoe.

Come, gentle May.

George James Webb, by per.

f Allegretto.

1. Come, gentle May! Come with thy robe of flowers; Come with thy sun and sky, thy
2. Come, gentle May! Come with thy mag - ic wand, Quick from the caverns of the

p

clouds and show'rs; Come, gentle May! Come with thy robe of flowers; Come with thy
breathing land; Come, gentle May! Come with thy mag - ic wand, Quick from the

f

sun and sky, thy clouds and show'rs; Come and bring forth un - to the light of
cav - erns of the breath - ing land; Come with thy green and ev - er bright ar -

From their...... im - pris'n - ing and mys - te - rious night,
That round..... thy foot - steps spring a - long the way,

day, From their im - pris'ning, their im - pris'ning and mys - te - rious night, The
ray, That round thy footsteps, round thy footsteps spring a - long the vale, While

From their im - pris'n - ing and mys - te - rious night,
That round thy foot - steps spring a - long the way,

buds of ma - ny hues, the children of thy light, The buds of ma - ny
glow - ing hearts and lips thy balm - y presence hail; While glowing hearts and

p Cres. f
hues, the children of thy light; Come. Come, Come, gen-tle May,
lips thy balmy presence hail; Come, Come, Come, gen-tle May,
Come,
Come with thy robe of flowers, Come with thy sun and sky, thy clouds and
Come with thy mag-ic wand, Quick from the cav-erns of the breath-ing
show'rs; Come, gentle May, Come with thy robe of flowers, Come with thy
land; Come, gentle May, Come with thy mag-ic wand, Quick from the
sun and sky, thy clouds and show'rs. Come, gen-tle May, Come, gen-tle
cav-erns of the breath-ing land.
Come, gentle May, gen-tle
May, Come, gen-tle May, Come, gen-tle May.
May, Come, gen-tle May, gen-tle May, Come, gen-tle May, gen-tle May.

O There's Music in the Waters.

Wm. Ross Wallace.

Wm. B. Bradbury, by per.

1. O there's mu - sic in the wa - ters, Play - ing on their sil - ver flutes,
2. O there's mu - sic in the cir - cle, Gathered round the household hearth,
3. O there's mu - sic in the can - non, Booming from the patriot host,
With the au - tumn's night-winds sigh - ing, Soft - ly o - ver air - y lutes;
Laughs of children, smiles of pa - rents, Sweetest bless - ings on the earth!
When the foe - men dare to tram - ple On Co - lum - bia's sa - cred coast;
There is mu - sic in the o - cean, Breaking on green isles a - far—
There is mu - sic in the greet - ing Of the moth - er, wife, or friend—
There is mu - sic in the wav - ing Of our flag on free - dom's cars—
Mu - sic in the sol - emn for - est— Mu - sic in the watching star!
Mu - sic of the times pro - phet - ic Where the song shall nev - er end.
Mu - sic, grand, tri - umphant mu - sic, In the rus - tle of its stars!
Chorus or Quartet.
We have list - ened to that mu - sic, Where the moon-lit wa - ters roll,
We have heard that house-hold mu - sic, Un - al - loyed by tin - sel art:
We have heard that might - y mu - sic, Sounding o - ver Freedom's goal;

And 'tis ours each tone to ech - o In the chambers of the soul:
How we glad - ly love to ech - o Tones like those un - to the heart:
Then hur - rah! and give their ech - oes Back to ev - ery free - man's soul:
And 'tis ours each tone to ech - o In the
How we glad - ly love to ech - o Tones like
Then hur - rah! and give their ech - oes Back to
cham - bers of the soul, In the cham - bers of the soul.
those un - to the heart, Tones like those un - to the heart!
ev - ery free - man's soul, Back to ev - ery free - man's soul!
Hark! the Merry Christ-Church Bells. Round.
1
Hark! the merry Christ church bells, One, two, three, four, five, six, They sound so
2
loud and deep, so clear and sweet, And they troul so mer-ri - ly, mer-ri-ly. Hark! the first and
sec - ond bell Which ev - ery day at four and ten, Cry come, come, come, come,
3
come to prayers, And the verger troops before the dean. Tingle, tingle, ting goes the small bell at nine, To
call the student home, But he'll never care To leave his chair, Till he hears the mighty Tom.

My Far-off Home.

Fanny J. Crosby. Theodore E. Perkins.

1. My
2. The
3. The
home, my ear - ly child - hood's home, Once more I come to
o - - range trees put forth their leaves, In ver - - nal beau - ty
flowers I trained with gen - tle hand, Will die without my
thee, ... Thy vine - clad hills and laugh - ing streams, Are
now, ... And birds their sweet - est car - - ols wake, From
care, ... And well I know, one trust - ing heart, Will

ev - er dear to me: And yet from all thy
eve - ry wav - - ing bough: Oh, no; I can - not
sad - ly miss me now: A - long those vales and
treas - ured scenes, In pen - sive thought I roam, Whose
lin - - ger here, Where once I loved to roam,— Then
sha - dy walks, I'd give the world to roam,— Then
Rallentando.

sil - ver fountains spar - kle bright, A - round the far - off home.
take me back, for mem - 'ry clings A - round the far - off home.
let me see, be - fore I die, My far - off, sun - ny home.

My Far-off Home. Concluded.

CHORUS.
p TENOR
Cres.
ff
pp
My far-off home, my far-off home, My far-off home, my far-off
ALTO
p SOPRANO
Cres.
ff
pp
My home, my home,...... my far-off home,........ my far-off
BASE.
My far-off home, my far-off home, My far-off home, my far-off
p
Cres.
ff
pp
Mezzo.
Ritard.
home, Then take me back, for mem'ry clings Around my home, my far-off, sunny home.
Mezzo.
Ritard.
home, Then take me back, for mem'ry clings Around my home, my far-off, sunny home.
Mezzo.
Ritard.

Teacher and Scholars.
TRIO.
I. B. Woodbury.
Pupils.
Fine.
Do, re, mi,
Do, si, do, O hear me, hear me;
Teacher.
Sit up e - rect, don't be a - fraid, To bend up dou-ble man nev-er was made;
Beat, beat the time, quickly and light, And then you nev-er need fear you're not right.
D. C.—Ah! what a rogue breaking the rule; I'll turn you, turn you right out of my school.
f
Ah, I love to sing with a fa la la,
Gen - - tly, gen - tly, don't you be so boisterous,
D. C.
Mer - ri - ly, mer - ri - ly, ha! ha! ha! ha! ha!
Ah! I see the rogue in yon - der cor - ner is the naughti - est;
Come, let us Learn to Sing.
Anon.
Wm. B. Bradbury.
Come, let us learn to sing, Do, re, mi, fa, so, la, si, do;
Loud let our voi - ces ring, Do, re, mi, fa, so, la, si, do;
Let us sing with o - pen sound,
With our voi - ces full and round, Do, si, la, so, fa, mi, re, do.
A Boat! a Boat to Cross the Ferry.
ROUND IN THREE PARTS.
1
2
A boat! a boat to cross the fer - ry, And while we
3
float sing hey down der - ry. And we'll go o - ver and be mer - ry.

Morning's Ruddy Beam.

G. LINLEY, arr.

Allegro.
1. Morning's rud-dy beam tints the east-ern sky,......... Up, com-rades, climb the mountain high;
Let the slug-gard sleep, we must slum-ber shun,........ Ere night-fall (Omit....................) hon-or must be won.
2. Eve-ning's gen-tle ray gilds the glow-ing west,........ Each hunt-er sighs for home and rest;
Hap-py in his toil, roam-ing blithe and free,........ O hunt-er, (Omit....................) thine's the life for me.
1st.
2d.
Haste, haste, haste, haste, the mer-ry bu-gle sounding, Chides our de-lay,....... chides our de-lay.
Haste, haste, haste, haste, o'er rock and gla-cier bounding, Soon each gal-lant hunt-er will sin-gle out his prey.
Haste, haste, haste, haste, with spoils in plenty la-den, Each one is stored,..... each one is stored.
Haste, haste, haste, haste, fond wife or anxious maid-en, Wait her gal-lant hunt-er a-round the humble board.
Morn-ing's rud-dy beam tints the east-ern sky,......... Up, com-rades, climb the moun-tain high;
Let the slug-gard sleep, we must slumber shun,......... Ere night-fall (Omit............................) hon-or must be won.
Eve-ning's gen-tle ray gilds the glowing west,......... Each hunt-er sighs for home and rest,
Hap-py in his toil, roam-ing blithe and free,.......... O hunt-er (Omit............................) thine's the life for me.
1st.
2d.

First time f, second time pp.
Tra la la la la la la, la la,
la la la la la:
Tra la la la la la la la la,
Tra la la la la la la, la la la la la la.
Repeat pp.
Tra la la la la la la,
Soft and Low.
Louis Spohr.
Andantino. p
1. Soft and low, I breathe my pas - sion, Will she wake and bless my sight;
2. Dost thou smile, my love dis - dain - ing, While in chill - ing mid-night's spite?
3. Far from love, o'er plain and riv - er, Late I rushed in head-long flight;
4. Leave me not in dark-ness pin - ing, From thy cur - tain'd win-dow's height:
Ah! if dreams her form might fash - ion, How un - wel - come were the light;
Here I wait, of thee com - plain-ing To the stars so cold and bright?
Oh! he fol - lowed ev - er, ev - er, Vain is speed a - gainst his might;
Let one look of pit - y shin - ing, Warm my heart to new de - light:
Fair - est, speak, and say good night, And say good night.
Oh! re - lent! and say good night, And say good night.
Here I yield! Oh! one good night, Oh! one good night.
Let me hear One sweet good night, One sweet good night.

The Dream of Home.

Andante con espressione.
T. J. Cook, by per.
1. Who has not felt how sad - ly sweet The dream of home, the dream of home,
2. Go, ask the sai - lor youth, when far His light bark bounds o'er ocean's home,
Steals o'er the heart so soon to fleet, When far o'er sea or land we roam?
What charms him most when evening star Smiles o'er the wave? to dream of home.
Sun-light more swift may o'er us fall, To greener shores our bark may come,
Fond tho'ts of absent friends and loves, At that sweet hour a - round him come,
But far more light, more dear than all, The dream of home, the dream of home.
His heart's best wish wher - e'er he roves, The dream of home, the dream of home.
Sweet the Pleasures. Round.
W. B. B.
Sweet the pleas-ures of the spring, When we hear the cuck-oo sing:
Cuckoo! Cuckoo! Cuckoo! Cuckoo! When we hear the cuck - oo sing.
Hark! hark! hark! Cuckoo! Cuckoo! Cuckoo! Hear the cuckoo sing.

The Sweet Voice.

GRACE J. FRANCES.
HUBERT P. MAIN, by per.
1. I dreamed that a - far I had wandered, And stood on a des - ert a - lone;
2. The cares of my life in a mo - ment Were lost in a thrill of de - light;
3. That voice in my heart I will cher - ish, And, when I am sad and op - pressed,
A voice o'er my spir - it came steal - ing; How soft its mag - ic - al tone!
The des - ert transformed to a gar - den, Where all was love - ly and bright.
Its ech - o, per - haps in my slum - ber, Will calm my sor - row to rest.
CHORUS.
Sweet voice,.... sweet voice,.... Dear, lov - ing voice! Where, where is the
Sweet voice, sweet voice, sweet voice, sweet voice,
bliss it gave? Why is the vis - ion o'er? Sweet voice,..... sweet voice,..... That
Sil - ver voice, sil - ver voice,
made my inmost soul rejoice! Oh say, was it all a dream? Gone to return no more?

Katy Did! Katy Did'nt!

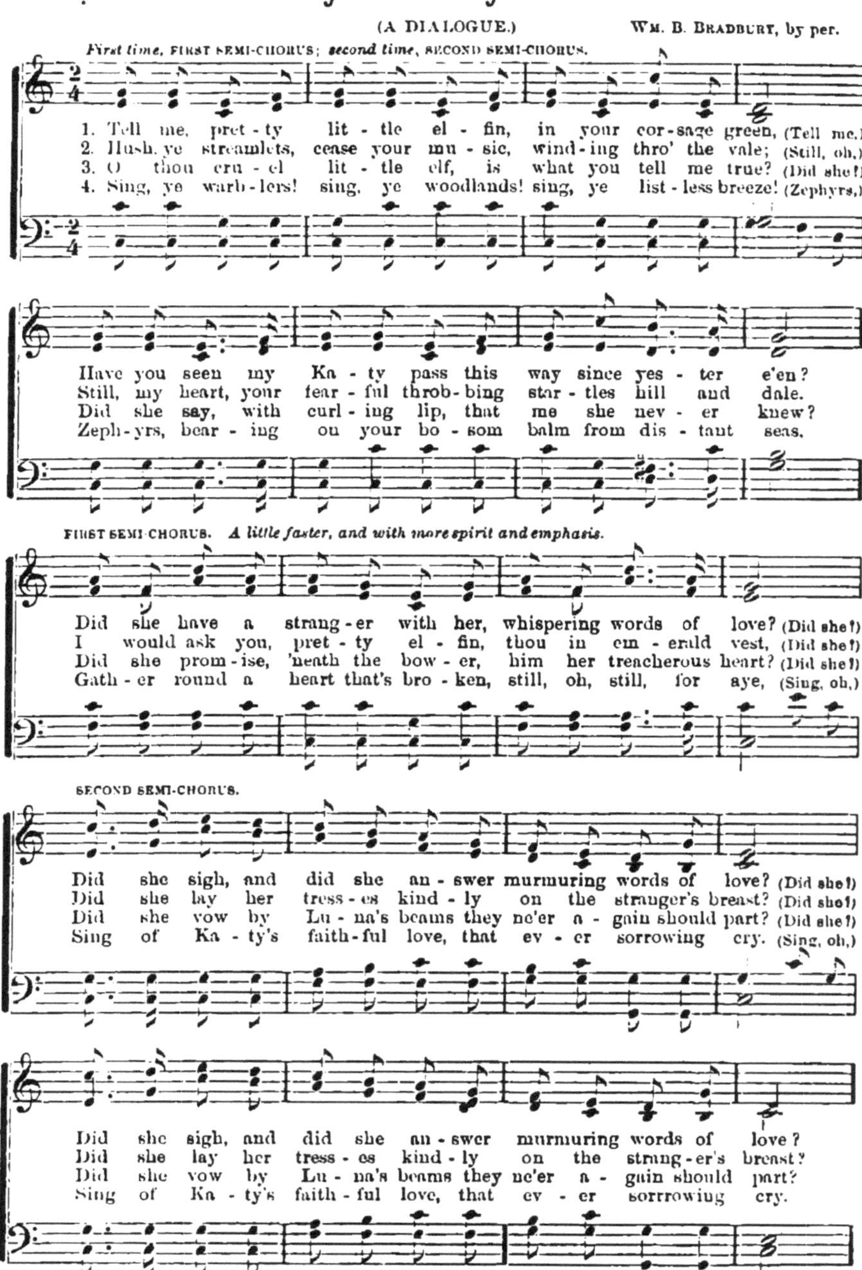
(A DIALOGUE.)
WM. B. BRADBURY, by per.
First time, FIRST SEMI-CHORUS; second time, SECOND SEMI-CHORUS.
1. Tell me, pret - ty lit - tle el - fin, in your cor-sage green, (Tell me,)
2. Hush, ye streamlets, cease your mu - sic, wind - ing thro' the vale; (Still, oh,)
3. O thou cru - el lit - tle elf, is what you tell me true? (Did she?)
4. Sing, ye warb - lers! sing, ye woodlands! sing, ye list - less breeze! (Zephyrs,)
Have you seen my Ka - ty pass this way since yes - ter e'en?
Still, my heart, your fear - ful throb - bing star - tles hill and dale.
Did she say, with curl - ing lip, that me she nev - er knew?
Zeph - yrs, bear - ing on your bo - som balm from dis - tant seas,
FIRST SEMI-CHORUS. A little faster, and with more spirit and emphasis.
Did she have a strang - er with her, whispering words of love? (Did she?)
I would ask you, pret - ty el - fin, thou in em - erald vest, (Did she?)
Did she prom - ise, 'neath the bow - er, him her treacherous heart? (Did she?)
Gath - er round a heart that's bro - ken, still, oh, still, for aye, (Sing, oh,)
SECOND SEMI-CHORUS.
Did she sigh, and did she an - swer murmuring words of love? (Did she?)
Did she lay her tress - es kind - ly on the stranger's breast? (Did she?)
Did she vow by Lu - na's beams they ne'er a - gain should part? (Did she?)
Sing of Ka - ty's faith - ful love, that ev - er sorrowing cry. (Sing, oh,)
Did she sigh, and did she an - swer murmuring words of love?
Did she lay her tress - es kind - ly on the strang - er's breast?
Did she vow by Lu - na's beams they ne'er a - gain should part?
Sing of Ka - ty's faith - ful love, that ev - er sorrowing cry.

FIRST SEMI-CHORUS.
SECOND SEMI-CHORUS.
"Yes, she did, Ka - ty did, Ka - ty did - n't! Ka - ty did - n't!
Ka - ty did! Ka - ty did - n't Ka - ty did— she did!

O Wipe away that Tear, Love.

GERMAN.

1. O, wipe a - way that tear, love, The pearl - y drop I see; Let hope thy bo - som cheer, love, Let hope thy bo - som cheer, love, As yon bright star we see.
2. Yes, when a - way from thee, love, Sweet hope shall be my star; We do not part for aye, love, We do not part for aye, love, I'll wel - come thee a - far.
3. At close of part - ing day, love, Ere yon bright star is set; Still meet me while a - way, love, Still meet me while a - way, love, 'Mid scenes we'll ne'er for - get.
4. I'll watch the set - ting star, love, And think I look on thee; And thus, tho' sun - dered far, love, And thus, tho' sun - dered far, love, How near our hearts may be.

Early Morning.

F. KÜCKEN.

1. Come forth this dawning ear - ly, La la la, ... la la, The
2. The east - ern clouds are light-er, La la la, ... la la, The
3. The morning blush is pal - ing, La la la, la la la, la la, The
dew is bright and pearl - y, La la la, ... la la, The
sky - blue arch is brighter, La la la la la la la, la la, The
morn-ing star is fail - ing, La la la la la la la, la la, The
morn-ing star is blink - - ing, The bees have left their hive, And
cat - tle all are low - - ing, To taste their hill - side fare, And
charms of youth and beau - ty Like morn will soon be gone; A -
wak - ing flowers are wink-ing, And birds are all a - live;.... The
chan - ti - cleer is crow-ing, Lone maidens drove them there;... And
wake to love and du - - - ty, A - wake, and hail the dawn; A -
wak - ing flowers are wink - ing, And birds are all a -
chan - ti - cleer is crow - ing, Lone maid - ens drove them
wake to love and du - - - ty, A - wake, and hail the

live. La la la la, la la la la la, la la la
there.
dawn. La la la la, la la la la, la la la la
la, la, la la la, la la la la la la, la la la.
la la, la la la la, la la la la, la la la la la.
God Speed the Right.
W. E. Hickson.
German.
Maestoso.
1. Now to heaven our prayer ascend - ing, God speed the right; In a no - ble
2. Be that prayer a - gain re - peat - ed—God speed the right; Ne'er de - spairing,
3. Pa - tient, firm, and per - se - ver - ing; God speed the right; Ne'er th'event nor
cause contend - ing, God speed the right. Be our zeal in heaven re - cord - ed,
though de-feat - ed, God speed the right. Like the good and great in sto - ry,
dan - ger fear - ing, God speed the right. Pains, nor toils, nor tri - als heed-ing,
With suc-cess on earth re - warded, God speed the right, God speed the right.
If we fail, we fail with glo - ry, God speed the right, God speed the right.
In the strength of heaven succeeding—God speed the right, God speed the right.

The Old Black Cat.

R. L.
ROBERT LOWRY.
1. Who so full of fun and glee, Hap-py as a cat can be? Polished sides so
2. Some will like the tortoise shell, Others love the white so well; Let them choose of
3. When the boys, to make her run, Call the dogs and set them on, Quickly I put
Affetuoso.
nice and fat—Oh, how I love the old black cat. Poor kit - ty! O, poor
this or that, But give to me the old black cat.
on my hat, And fly to save the old black cat.
CHORUS.
kit - ty! Sit - ting so co - sy Un - der the stove. Pleas-ant, pur - ring,
pret-ty pus - sy, Fris - ky, full of fun, and fus - sy, Mor - tal foe of
mouse and rat, O, I love the old black cat, Yes, I do.

Good Night. (Trio.)

Mrs. C. G. Goodwin.
Wm. B. Bradbury, by per.
SOPRANO.
And now, be - fore we part, we'll say good night, We'll
ALTO.
And now be- fore we part, we'll say once more good night, we'll say once more good night, good night, We'll
BASE.
And now, be - fore we part, we'll say good night, We'll
say once more good night, good night, good night. Good
say once more good night, good night, good night, good night, good night, good night. Good
say once more good night, good night, good night. Good
night to all, Sweet - ly sleep till morn-ing light, Good
night, good night to all, good night, good night to all, good night, good night, good night, good night, good
night to all, Sweet - ly sleep till morn-ing light, Good
Repeat pp.
night to all, good night, good night, good night.
night, good night to all, good night, good night to all, good night, good night.
night to all, good night, good night, good night.

In Thy Lonely Path Descending.

F. J. C.
HUMMEL, arr. by C. G. ALLEN.
1. In thy lone - ly path de - scend-ing, From the dis - tant mountain's brow,
2. All is si - lent!—like a shad - ow Thou art glid - ing o'er the lea;
Guard, O Night, our tran - quil slumber, Fold thy man - tle o'er me now:
Wel - come, Night, in peace re - turn - ing, Pleasant mem - 'ries come with thee:
Through the part - ed leaves that trem-ble, Light - ly sway - ing to and fro,
Veiled in beau - ty, robed in splendor, Bear us far in dreams a - way,
Star - ry eyes are mild - ly beam - ing On the sleep - ing vale be - low.
Till the o - rient sky is glow - ing With the crim - son blush of day.
CHORUS.
In thy lone - ly path de - scend-ing, From the dis - tant mountain's brow,

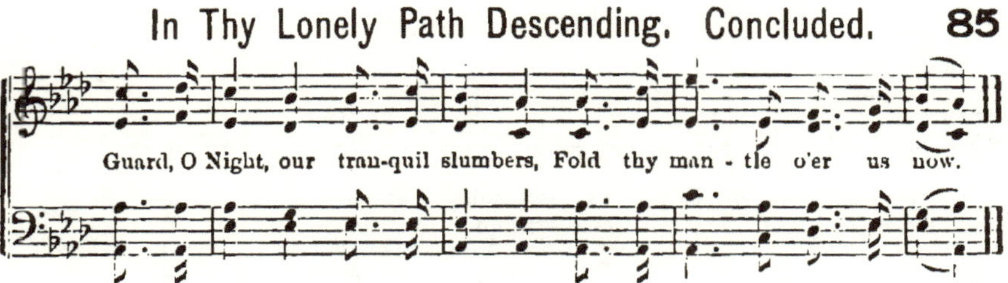
Guard, O Night, our tran-quil slumbers, Fold thy man - tle o'er us now.

Awake! the Starry Midnight Hour.

BRYAN W. PROCTER. MENDELSSOHN.

1. A - wake! the star - ry mid - night hour, Hangs charm'd, and paus-eth
2. A - wake! soft dews will soon a - rise, From dai - sied mead and

in its flight; A - wake! A - wake! A - wake! A - wake! In
thorn - y brake; A - wake! A - wake! A - wake! A - wake! Then

its own sweet - ness sleeps the flow'r; And doves lie hushed in
sweet, un - cloud those east - ern eyes, And like the ten - der

deep de - light! A - wake! A - wake! Look forth, my love, for love's sweet sake!
morn - ing, break! A - wake! A - wake! Dawn forth, my love, for love's sweet sake!

Merry May.

FANNY J. VAN ALSTYNE.
HUBERT P. MAIN, by per.
Lively.
1. While ver - dure crowns our na - tive hills, And blooms in ev - ery vale,
2. Young hope has twined for ev - ery brow, A ro - sy gar - land gay,
3. How kind the hand that decks the field, And makes the lil - y bloom,
The woods are ring - ing with de - light, There's joy in ev - ery gale.
While pleas- ure comes with ge - nial light And cheer - ful smiles to - day.
That gives the rose its silk - en leaves, The bird its crest - ed plume.
The brook that spar - kles in the dell, Goes laugh-ing on its way,
Oh! we are hap - py as the birds, That in the wood - land sing,
O may our hearts in ear - ly youth, To that dear Friend be given,
And all re - joice to hear a - gain, The song of mer - ry May.
For, like our sun - ny childhood years, No sea - son like the Spring.
So may we live for Him on earth, And dwell with Him in heaven.
CHORUS.
Then welcome, wel - come, gen - tle Spring, With buds and blossoms fair;

Merry May. Concluded.
87
There's beau - ty in the for - est now, And mu - sic ev - ery - where.
Wake up, Little Daisy.
Mrs. Mary A. Kidder.
Sprightly.
Wm. B. Bradbury, by per.
1. Wake up, lit - tle dai - sy, the sum - mer is nigh, The dear lit - tle rob - in is up in the sky, The snow-drop and cro - cus are nev - er so slow; Then wake up, lit - tle dai - sy, and has - ten to grow.
2. I ask pleasant sunshine to rest on your head, The dew and the raindrops to moisten your bed; And then ev - ery morning I just take a peep, To see your lit - tle face, but you're still fast a - sleep.
3. Moth - er oft - en tells me, "if I would be wise, And hon - ored, and hap - py, I ear - ly must rise;" So I'm up in the morning, and out in the dew, With all the lit - tle birds, and the hon - ey bees too.
4. List - en, lit - tle dai - sy, I'll whis - per what's said;—The lark thinks you're la - zy, and love your warm bed; But I'll not be - lieve it, for now I can see Your bright lit - tle eye soft - ly wink - ing at me.
p
f
Wake up, Wake up, Wake up, lit - tle dai - sy, and has - ten to grow.
Wake up, Wake up,

Night.

Moderately.
TRIO FOR FEMALE VOICES.
FRANZ ABT.
1st SOPRANO.
2d SOPRANO.
ALTO.
1. Soft - ly roam, gen - tle night; O'er the fields with dew impearled; Smile in tranquil
2. Pure and clear, calm, be - nign, See yon gold - en evening star; Lord, is this a
star - ry light, On the si - lent, sleeping world! Sickness and sor - row hush them to
glance of Thine, Darkness scatt'ring near and far? Heaven-ly splen - dor light us to
SOLO. mf
rest; Bless us, and rock us in dreams on thy breast; Sickness and
rest; Fa - ther, dear Fa - ther, keep us still blest; Heav - en - ly
mf TUTTI.
sor - row hush them to rest; Bless us, and rock... us in dreams on thy breast.
splendor, light us to rest; Fa - ther, dear Fa - ther, keep us still blest.

The Spring-time is Coming.

FANNY J. CROSBY.
THEODORE E. PERKINS, by per.
1. The spring-time is com - ing, the win - ter is past, Beau - ty and
2. The blue - birds are com - ing, from is - lands that sleep, Rocked on its
3. The dew - drops are com - ing, re - fresh - ing the bowers, Fall - ing like
4. The zeph - yrs are com - ing, and what do they bring? O - dors, sweet
sun - shine are blend - ing at last; And see, a - long the
bo - som, the foam - crest - ed deep; And with the laugh - ing
pearls on the leaves and the flowers, And steal - ing where the
o - dors, to wel - come the spring: All na - ture wakes the
gras - sy plain, Dai - sies are bloom-ing a - gain. Dai - sies white and
dai - sies sing, Beau - ti - ful, beau - ti - ful Spring.
dai - sies sleep, Lov - ing - ly, gent - ly they weep.
tune - ful strain, Dai - sies are bloom-ing a - gain.
dai - sies rare, Pure as the blush of the morn - ing;
Dai - sies white and dai - sies fair, Pure as the blush of the morn.

Evening Bells.

Fanny J. Crosby. Wm. F. Sherwin, by per.

1. Eve-ning bells, oh! eve-ning bells, Peal-ing thro' the qui-et dells;
2. Eve-ning bells, I tread a-lone Where, in years that now have flown,
3. Eve-ning bells, I lin-ger yet, Not to weep with vain re-gret,
Rit.
Sweet the tale your mu-sic tells, Float-ing on the breeze a-long.
Oft I heard your sil-ver tone, Peal-ing on the twi-light air.
Tho' my soul can ne'er for-get How I loved your hap-py chime;
While a-mong these rus-tic bowers I am dreaming— fond-ly dreaming,
Still for those I treas-ured then, I am pin-ing, ev-er pin-ing;
Once a-gain your mu-sic pour, Gently swell-ing— rap-ture tell-ing,
Rit.
Falls the light of van-ished hours, Mem'ries sweet of love and song.
Where is now that youthful train? Bells of evening, tell me where?
Joy my heart may feel no more, Evening bells of old-en time.
Eve - - - ning bells! Eve - - - ning bells!
Eve-ning bells, O eve-ning bells, Peal-ing thro' the qui-et dells,
Eve - - - ning bells! Eve - - - ning bells!

Ritardando.
Sweet the tale your mu-sic tells, Float-ing on the breeze a-long.
Eve - - - - ning bells! ...... Float - ing a - - - long.

Hear the Warbling Notes.

THEO. F. SEWARD, by per.

1. Hear the warbling notes of spring-time, From the gay and cheer-ful throng, Ev-ery
2. Hear the ech - oes as they're ring-ing, Far and near, o'er hill and dale, Let us

La la la la la la la la la la la la la la la,

Stac.
voice is filled with gladness, Let us join their happy, happy song. La la la la la la la
join them in our singing, Sending forth our songs in every gale.

la la la, la la la, la la la la la.

f
la la la, Hear the ech-oes so gai-ly ring-ing, La la la la la la la

1st. 2d.
la la la la la la la la la la la la la la. la la.

Where the Sparkling Waters Play.

Grace J. Frances. DUET & CHORUS. Hubert P. Main, by per.

1. Where the spark - ling wa-ters play, Laughing, danc - ing all the
2. Where the swal - low from her nest, Calls her ten - - der brood to
3. Where the mu - - sic of the breeze, Gent - ly floats a-mong the
day: Where my skiff may safe - ly glide...... O'er a
rest, Fold - ing each be - neath her wings,..... While her
trees, While a - mid the boughs of green,..... Moonlight

Published as a Duet for Soprano and Contralto in sheet form by Spear & Dehnhoff.

With its snow - - - white
With the min - - - strel
'Tis a ma - - - gic

calm........ and peace-ful tide:...... With its white, its snow - white
lul - - - la - by she sings;..... With the minstrel, min - strel
hangs....... her sil - ver sheen;..... 'Tis a ma-gic, ma - gic

sail,..... In the laugh - - - ing gale:..... There is
throng,.. In their ves - - - - per song,..... How I
hour. ... And I feel.......... its power,... There is

sail,..... In the laugh-ing. laugh - ing gale:..... There is
throng,.. In their ves - per, ves - per song,..... How I
hour,.... And I feel, I feel its power,... There is

joy.. ... for me,...... There is joy...... for me......
long..... to be,....... How I long..... to be......
joy...... for me,...... There is joy...... for me......

joy, is joy for me,...... There is joy, is joy for me......
long, I long to be,....... How I long, I long to be .,....
joy, is joy for me,...... There is joy, is joy for me......

CHORUS.
Where the sweet - - est flow - rets grow, And the
pur - - - est zeph - yrs blow; How I love..... to roam in my
Cantabile.
for - est home, By the wa - ters murm - 'ring low.
Ritardando. pp
murm'ring, murm'ring

Song of the Brook.

Words by Maydew.
Theodore E. Perkins, by per.
1. Mer-ry wa-ters, leap-ing—flow-ing, On-ward to the riv-er go-ing,
2. Mer-ry wa-ters, leap-ing—flow-ing, Thro' your i-cy chan-nels go-ing,
3. Mer-ry wa-ters, leap-ing—flow-ing, Naught of sad-ness ev-er know-ing,
Nev-er wait-ing— nev-er wea-ry, Nev-er sad and nev-er drea-ry;
Summer days have long de-part-ed, Why are you still hap-py-heart-ed?
All my heart is full of sor-row, Dark and dark-er looms to-mor-row—
Tell me why you laugh for-ev-er, Hur-ry-ing on to join the riv-er?
Tell me, as you leap and quiv-er, Hur-ry-ing on to join the riv-er?
Tell me, in your mys-tic measure, How can grief be linked with pleas-ure?
Chorus.
Rip-pling, roll-ing, danc-ing on, Heark-en to the brooklet's song:
Repeat p.
"Sum-mer comes when win-ter's gone!" Thus it sings the whole day long.

I Am Dreaming.

FANNY J. CROSBY. Mrs. MARY C. SEWARD, by per.

1. I am dream - - ing of a cot-tage, Half con-cealed beneath the
2. I am dream - - ing, fondly dreaming Of a blue - - - eyed maiden
p
1. I am dreaming of a cot-tage, Half conceal d beneath the
2. I am dreaming, fondly dreaming Of a blue eyed maiden
shade, Where the rob - - - ins sweet-ly caroled, And the i - - dle zeph-yr
fair, With her cheeks, of mer-ry dimples And a step as light as
shade, Where the robins sweetly caroled, And the i - dle zeph-yr
fair. With her cheeks of merry dimples, And a step as light as
played, And I weep as o'er me stealing Comes an ech - - o soft and
air; But we laid her with the ros - es, Where a brook - let murmurs
p
played; La la la la la la la la la
air;
low, From a lute whose chords were broken,
low, And my life's young love is sleeping,
Cres.
la la la la la la la la, By the touch of long a -
In the grave of long a -
Dim.
Still in pen - - - sive thought I
go, By the touch of long a - go. Still in pensive thought I
go, In the grave of long a - go.

lin - ger, By that rus - tic cot - tage door, But the
lin - ger, By that rus - tic cot - tage door,
zeph - - - - yr
But the zeph - yr moans in pit - y, And the rob - ins sing no more.
Rit.
Bye, Baby, Bye!
Mrs. Mary Mapes Dodge.
Hubert P. Main, by per.
Gently.
1. Bye, ba - by, day is o - ver, Bees are drows-ing in the
2. Bye, ba - by, birds are sleep-ing; One by one the stars are
3. Bye, ba - by, moth - er holds thee; Lov - ing, ten - der care en -
clo - ver; Bye, ba - by, bye! Now the sun to bed is glid - ing,
peep-ing; Bye, ba - by, bye! In the far - off sky they twin - kle,
folds thee; Bye, ba - by, bye! An - gels in thy dreams ca - ress thee;
All the pret - ty flowers are hid - ing— Bye, ba - by, by.
While the cows come tin - kle, tin - kle, Bye, ba - by, by.
Thro' the dark - ness guard and bless thee; Bye, ba - by, by.

The Falling Snow.

FANNY J. CROSBY. THEO. E. PERKINS, by per

In a flowing, easy manner.
1. Grace-ful - ly down, qui - et - ly down, Falls the white snow on the
2. Look at the hills, man-tled in snow, See how it falls in the
mead - ows so brown; Sum - mer has gone, au - tumn has fled,
val - ley be - low; O - ver the lawn, o - ver the plain,
All the sweet blossoms are dead: Look at the trees, frost-y and bright.
Winter is creeping a - gain: Hap - py are we, mer-ry are we,
FINE.
See how they spar - kle and wave in the light; O - ver the lawn,
Slid - ing a - way in our in - no - cent glee; O - ver the brook,

Light and Gay.

FANNY J. VAN ALSTYNE. HUBERT P. MAIN, by per

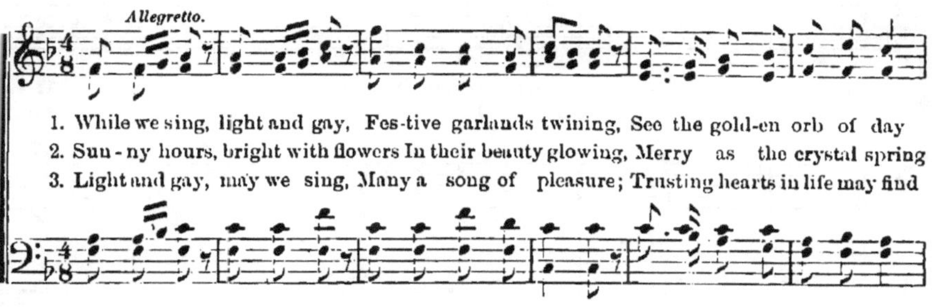
Allegretto.
1. While we sing, light and gay, Fes-tive garlands twining, See the gold-en orb of day
2. Sun - ny hours, bright with flowers In their beauty glowing, Merry as the crystal spring
3. Light and gay, may we sing, Many a song of pleasure; Trusting hearts in life may find

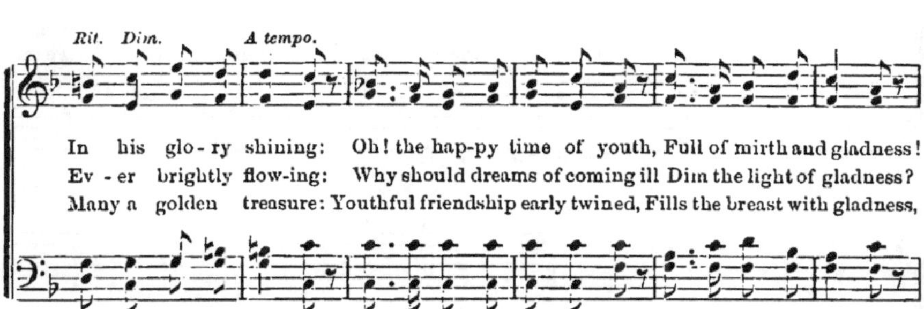
Rit. Dim.
A tempo.
In his glo - ry shining: Oh! the hap-py time of youth, Full of mirth and gladness!
Ev - er brightly flow-ing: Why should dreams of coming ill Dim the light of gladness?
Many a golden treasure: Youthful friendship early twined, Fills the breast with gladness,

Vivace.
Rit. Dim.
CHORUS.

Can it be that we shall know Care, and gloom, and sadness? Light and gay, while we sing,
Hope has still a smile to meet Every cloud of sad-ness.
Cheers it, tho' its chords may feel Grief, and pain, and sadness.

Vivace.
Rit. Dim.
Shouting, full of gladness; To the fu - ture let us leave Every thought of sadness.

100
Come, Schoolmates, with Me.
F. J. C.
Henry Tucker, by per.
1. Come, schoolmates, with me, Where the wild for - est free, Ar - rayed in its beau - ty, is hap - - py with glee; Oh, come while the day With its bright morn-ing ray, All the shad - ows from na - ture is chas - ing a - way.
2. How gent - ly the flowers In their glad summer bowers Are smil - ing to wel - come the young morn-ing hours; Then how can we stay? For they call us a - way, And the bright gold - en sun - shine a - waits us to - day.
Fine.
1. Cool zephyrs in - vite us, while, balm-y with o - dor, They come to us soft - ly in sun - shine and
2. Come, dance with the brooklet; come, sing with the foun-tain; Of ros - es and lil - ies a chap - let we'll
Come, come, come, come, come, come, Come, come, come, come, come, come,

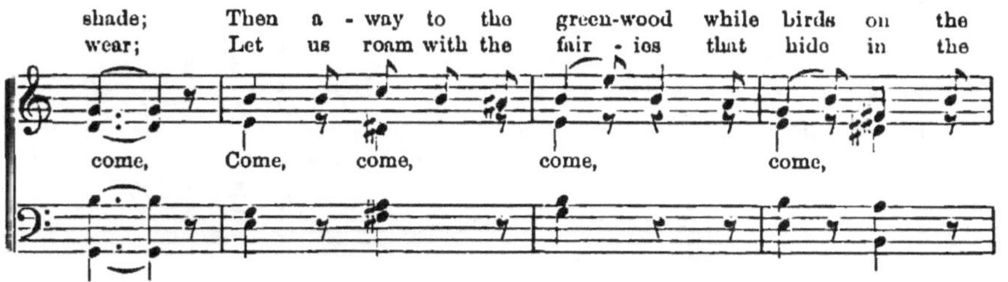
shade; Then a - way to the green-wood while birds on the
wear; Let us roam with the fair - ies that hide in the
come, Come, come, come, come,

wing,........ With their mu-sic are wak - ing the sweet mos - sy glade.
dell:........ Oh, the greenwood is love - ly, and we must be there.
D. C.
come, come, come, come, come, come, come, come; Ah,

As the Moon Shone Bright and Fair.

GABLER.

1. As the moon shone bright and fair, Ran a mer - ry lit - tle hare,
2. But he has not hit the hare, See! he's load - ing now with care,
3. Lit - tle hare, with mor - tal fear, Sprung be-hind the green-hedge near,
4. Then the moon her bright-ness veiled, 'Neath the clouds which o'er her sailed;
5. Lit - tle hare then went to bed, Coat and shoes placed by his head,

Look - ing for its eve - ning food,— Huntsman's shot rings through the wood.
Put - ting pow - der in the lead, "Lit - tle hare will soon be dead."
Begged the moon, "Put out your light, Hide me from the huntsman's sight."
Gather-ed clouds both great and small, Turn-ing light to dark - ness all.
Laid him down in moss so bright, Sound-ly slept till morn - ing light.

The Spring Bird.

FANNY J. CROSBY. HUBERT P. MAIN, by per.

Lively.

1. Come hith-er, come hith-er thou bird of the spring, And rest thee a - while on thy
2. Come hith-er, and hap-py thy dwelling shall be, These branches are covered with

bright crest-ed wing; I know thou art wea - ry, thy jour-ney was long, O
blos - soms for thee, A voice in each leaf-let thy wel-come will sing, Then

rest thee, and warble thy wild-wood song; Say where thou hast been thro' the long winter hours,
lin - ger, oh, linger thou bird of spring; A-wake me from sleep when the dawning of day

And what hast thou seen in the ev - er-green bowers That bloom on the isl - and of
Is chas - ing the darkness and shadows a - way; What visions of rap-ture thy

beau - ty, that sleep. Cra - dled and rocked in the arms of the deep?
mu - sic will bring, Lin - ger, oh, lin - ger thou bird of the spring.

pp Dim.

Sweet Evening Hour.

T. F. S.
KULLAK arr. by THEO. F. SEWARD.
pp Slow and soft.
1. O sweet evening hour, O calm and qui - et evening, How
1. Sweet eve - ning hour, sweet eve - - ning hour,
gent - ly thy power, From care each heart re-liev-ing, The birds to their nests with
2. From care each heart re-liev-ing, The stars one by one in
sweet hour.
p
f
cheer - ful songs re - tir - ing, All na - ture's glad voices come with sound in-spir - ing,
heav'ns blue vault are shining, The light zephyrs play where ros - es are entwin-ing,—
Dim.
Rit.
a tempo.
Come till all is hushed to rest. O sweet evening hour, O calm and qui - et
Fra - grance fling-ing ev - ery - where.
sweet eve - - ning
pp
Rit.
evening, How gentle thy power. O sweet evening hour, sweet evening hour, sweet hour.
sweet evening hour.
hour, sweet hour,

Give Welcome to the Swallow.

F. Kücken.
Duet.
1. Give welcome to the swal - low, He news of summer brings; A - cross the sea, a -
2. Ye lit-tle playful lamb - kins, Ye here can safe-ly stay, Ye fear no harm, with
3. Farewell, then, to the swal - low, He skims a - long the plain, The home he leaves be -
far comes he With sunshine on his wings. But when the leaves are fall - ing, No
fleece so warm, From winter's bit-ter day: But when the leaves are fall - ing, And
neath the eaves He soon will seek a - gain: But fast the leaves are fall - ing, He
lon - ger will he stay, But when the leaves are fall - ing, No lon - ger
bar - ren is the spray, But when the leaves are fall - ing, And bar - ren
can not lin - ger here, But fast the leaves are fall - ing, He can not

will be stay, He hur-ries past, from win-ter's
is the spray, The swallow flies to brighter
lin - - ger here; When sweet birds sing, in ear-ly
He hurries past, from winter's blast,
The swallow flies to brighter skies,
When sweet birds sing, in ear-ly spring,
blast, Far, far a - way, far,
skies, Far, far a - way, far,
spring, He will ap - pear, he,
He hur-ries past, from win-ter's blast, He hur - ries
Far, far a - way; the swallow flies, To brighter
He will ap - pear; when sweet birds sing, In ear - ly
far.................... a - way: He flies a -
far.................... a - way: He flies a -
will .... ap - pear: When sweet birds
past; From winter's blast he flies a - way, Far, far a - way:
skies, The swallow flies to bright-er skies. Far, far a - way:
spring, He will ap - pear, he will ap - pear, When sweet birds sing:

way, Far, far a - way, far,
way, Far, far a - way, far,
sing, He will ap - pear, he
From win-ter's blast, He hur-ries past f.om win - ter's
The swallow flies, The swa-low flies to bright-er
He will ap - pear, In ear - ly spring, when sweet birds
far........................... a - way, From....... win - ter's
far........................... a - way, To......... brighter
will........................... ap - pear, When....... sweet birds
blast, He hur-ries past, Far, far a - way, From....... win - ter's
skies, He flies a - way. Far, far a - way, To....... brighter
sing. He will ap - pear, He will ap - pear, When....... sweet birds
blast He........ hur-ries past, Far, far a - way..........
skies He........ flies a - way, Far, far a - way..........
sing, He........ will ap - pear, He will ap - pear.........

Star of the Evening.

Theodore E. Perkins, by per.

1. Star of the eve - ning, Glo - ry on high,...... Queen of the beau - ti - ful, Gem of the sky: Light of the trav - el - er, Longing for rest, Ev - er - more peace - ful - ly Glow in the west.
2. Eyes that are watch - ing, Gaze up - on thee,...... Eyes that are anx - ious - ly Watch - ing for me; Joy of the wan - der - er, Ev - er - more shine, Smiling I gaze on thee, Smile thou on mine.
3. Day star of glad - ness, When o'er the skies,...... Tem - pests and dark - ness sweep, Do thou a - rise; And when faith fail - eth us, Light of the blest, Shine on our wan - der - ings, Guide us to rest,
Chorus.
Star of the eve - ning, Glo - ry on high, Queen of the beau - ti - ful, Gem of the sky.

Rain on the Roof.

COL. COATES KINNEY. CHORUS & QUARTET. ISAAC B. WOODBURY. 1856.

1. When the hu - mid show-ers gath - er O - ver all the star - ry spheres,
2. Ev - ery tin - kle on the shingles Has an ech - o in the heart,
3. There is naught in art's bra - vu - ras That can work with such a spell,
La la la la la la la la la la la la la la la la la
And the mel - an - cho - ly dark - ness Gent - ly weeps in rain - y tears, 'Tis a
And a thousand dream - y fan - cies In - to bus - y be - ing start; And a
In the spir - it's pure, deep fountains, Whence the ho - ly passions swell, As that
la la la la la la la la la la la la la la la.
Cres.
joy to press the pil - low Of a cot - tage-cham - ber bed, And to
thousand re - col - lec - tions Weave their bright hues in - to woof, As I
mel - o - dy of na - ture, That sub - dued, sub - du - ing strain, Which is
lis - ten to the pat - ter Of the soft rain o - ver - head. La la
lis - ten to the pat - ter Of the soft rain on the roof.
play'd up - on the shingles By the pat - ter of the rain.
La la la la la,
la la la la la la la la, la la la la la......................
la la la la la la la la, la la la la la la.

Merrily Gliding On.

Fanny J. Crosby.
Hubert P. Main, by per.
1. The moon is up, the winds are still, The waves, in i - dle play Now curl a-round the
2. We leave the cool and sha-dy grot Where elves and fairies hide, And wake the myriads
3. Ah! dearer far than morning beams These moonlight hours we prize; Where love, its glance like
dripping oar, While glides our boat a - way: Then light - ly row, yes, light - ly row, Let
from their sleep Beneath the sparkling tide: There's not a breath dis-turbs the deep, No
ar - row throws From merry, laughing eyes: A - way, a - way, the wa - ter's blue, To
mu-sic's hap-py chime In tune - ful num-bers float a-long, And heart and voice keep time.
dreaded storm is near; There's not a cloud in yon-der arch So lov - ing, calm and clear.
mirth and song invite; And ev - ery star its beauty lends To speed us on to-night.
Refrain.
We're glid-ing, glid-ing, glid-ing; Oh, gen - tly ply the oar. We're
glid-ing, glid-ing, glid-ing, Mer - ri - ly glid - ing from the shore.

Morning in the Alpine Vale.

Arranged from NAEGELI.
1. See, as morn - ing light is beam - ing, O'er the spark - - ling gla - cier
2. While the mer - ry peals are chim - ing, Cheerful shep - - herd boys are
gleam-ing, Night creeps slow to cav-erns drear. Wak - ing birds are gai - ly
climb-ing, Where bright Al - pine grass is seen. Horns are sound - ing, sheep-bells
sing-ing, Morning bells are sweetly ring-ing, Sing-ing, ring - ing, far and
ring-ing, Goats are climbing, lambs are springing, Kine are crop - ing herb-age
Morn - ing bells, &c.
far and near..........
near, Singing, ring-ing, far and near, Sing-ing, ring - ing, far and near.
green, Kine are cropping herb - age green, Kine are crop - ping herbage green.
far and near..........

3 Strong-armed mowers, waking early,
Dash the dew-drops, bright and pearly,
As they climb with sturdy feet.
Songs are sounding, scythes are blinking,
Leaves are falling, leaves are sinking,
Redolent of odors sweet.

4 Far above, with weapon ready,
Climbs the hunter, strong and steady,
Leaping chasms deep and wide.
Shots are echoing and resounding,
Chamois down the rocks are bounding,
Low is brought the eagle's pride.

5 Warming sunshine, skies of azure,
Balmy airs, imparting pleasure;
How can sorrow here be known.
Life of freedom, sweet employment,
Peaceful rest, and pure enjoyment,
Subject to the Lord alone.

Sweet and Low

Alfred Tennyson.
Joseph Barnby.
pp Larghetto.
1. Sweet and low, Sweet and low Wind of the wes - tern sea, Low, low, breathe and blow, Wind of the wes - tern sea, O - ver the roll - ing wa - ters go; Come from the dy - ing moon and blow, Blow him a - gain to me, While my lit - tle one, while my pret - ty one sleeps.
2. Sleep and rest, Sleep and rest Fa - ther will come to thee soon; Rest, rest on moth - er's breast, Fa - ther will come to thee soon, Fa-ther will come to his babe in the nest; Sil - ver sails all out of the west, Un - der the sil - ver moon: Sleep my lit - tle one, sleep my pret - ty one, sleep.
mf
Rall e dim.
Come, Come, Follow. (Round.)
Come, come, fol - low, fol - low, fol - low, fol - low, fol - low, fol - low me;
Whither shall I fol - low, fol-low, fol-low, whither shall I fol - low, fol-low thee?
To the greenwood, greenwood, greenwood, To the beau - ti - ful greenwood tree.

Hail our Country's Natal Morn.

Wm. Gilmore Simms.
CHORUS FOR THE FOURTH OF JULY.
I. B. Woodbury.
Very spirited.
1. Hail our country's na - tal morn! Hail, our spreading kindred born, Hail thou banner,
2. Who would sever freedom's shrine? Who would draw th'invidious line? Tho' by birth one
3. By our al - tars pure and free, By our laws' deep-root-ed tree, By the past's dread
4. Fathers! have ye bled in vain? A - ges! must ye droop again? Mak-er! shall we
not yet torn, Wav-ing o'er the free! While this day in festal throng, Millions swell the
spot be mine, Dear is all the rest: Dear to me the South's fair land, Dear the central
mem-o - ry, By our Washing-ton: By our common parent tongue, By our hopes, bright,
rash - ly stain Blessings sent by Thee? No! re - ceive our sol-emn vow, While before thy
pa - triot's song, Shall not we thy notes pro-long, Hal - lowed Ju - bi - lee?
mountain band, Dear New-England's rock - y strand, Dear the prai - ried West.
buoy-ant young, By the tide of country strong, We will still be One.
throne we bow, Ev - er to maintain as now "U - nion— Lib - er - ty!"
O, Ye Tears!
Franz Abt.
Andantino.
mf
1. O, ye tears, O, ye tears, that have long re - fused to flow, Ye are
2. O, ye tears, O, ye tears, I am thank-ful that you run, Tho' ye
Con espress.
wel - come to my heart, thawing, thawing like the snow; The ice-bound clod has
come from cold and dark, ye shall glit - ter in the sun: The rain-bow can - not

yielded, and the ear - ly snow-drops spring, And the heal-ing fountains gush, and the wil - der-ness shall sing, O, ye tears, O, ye tears.
cheer us, if the show'rs re - fuse to fall, And the eyes that can - not weep are the sad - dest eyes of all, O, ye tears,
p
The Snow Birds.
Arr by FLORENCE LE CLARE.
MEHUL, arr. by H. R. PALMER, by per.
1. When winter winds are blowing, And clouds are full of snow, Then comes a flock of birdlings A - fly - ing to and fro, A - bout the with-ered gar - den, A - round the na - ked field, The trees of hedge or way-side, That may a ber - ry yield.
2. But when the snow-drifts cover The gar - den and the field, When shrubs and trees are i - cy, And ev - ery brook is sealed, Then come the lit - tle snow-birds, As beg-gars to your door; They pick each crumb so ti-ny, With ea - ger chirps for more.
3. Like wander - ing mu-sicians, They 'neath the window sing, All thro' the long, cold win - ter, But leave us in the Spring, Off to the land of ice-bergs; To is - lands cold and drear, They fly, ere comes the Summer, To frol - ic with us here.
4. You see them flit - ting, flitting, And hear their mer-ry song; The crumbs of Summer's feast-ing, Feed win - ter bird-lings long. Give them a heart-y wel - come; It sure - ly were not good That they who sing in win - ter Should ev-er lack for food.

We Tune our Happy Voices.

GRACE J. FRANCES. HUBERT P. MAIN.

CHORUS FOR BOYS.

1. We tune our hap-py voi-ces, We hail these fes-tive hours, Bright gems of flor-al beau-ty We bring from syl-van bowers.
2. Come, join our hap-py cho-rus, Come, swell our mer-ry lay, Till all the ech-oes wak-ing, Shall bear it far a-way.
3. Young hearts are light-ly bounding, Glad songs of joy we hear, And see, the sky a-bove us, How love-ly, bright and clear.

TRIO. 1st & 2d TREBLE & ALTO.

Our flor-al gems may lan-guish, Ere half the day is o'er, The buds that smell the sweet-est, May bloom for us no more, And
There's not a leaf-let mov-ing, The sul-try air is still, The birds their wings are lav-ing, In yon-der glas-sy rill; The
But threat'ning clouds may gath-er, And fill our hearts with dread, And peals of roll-ing thun-der, A fear-ful ru-in spread; From

ACCOMP.

thus our pur - est pleas - ures Are like a pass - ing
flee - cy lambs are pant - ing, That in the mead - ow
eyes that smile the bright - est, The sad - dest tears may
Rit.
dream, They come and then they van - ish, They are not what they seem.
played, Then do not tar - ry lon - ger, But find a cool - er shade.
flow, And hearts that beat the light - est, The deep - est grief may know.
SOLO, or CHORUS. GIRLS.
O come,................... We hail these fes - tive hours; Bright
FULL CHORUS.
Come, with songs of glad - ness, Hail these fes - tive hours;
ff
gems,................... We bring from syl - van bowers.
Gems of flor - al beau - ty, Bring from syl - van bowers.

Katie's Blushes.

THEO. D. C. MILLER, M. D.
H. P. DANKS, by per.
1. O Ka-ty dar-ling, Why hide your blushes? Those rosy flushes I love to see!
2. O Ka-ty dar-ling, My heart is pleading, And in-ter-ceeding Each hour with thee!
3. O Ka-ty dar-ling, Morning is breaking, My heart is waking Its bliss to see!
Why tease me longer— O cru-el blindness—In loving kindness Come love to me.
Then dear one whisper: 'Tis by thee tak-en In heart love spoken, I'll come to thee!
Then heed my calling, And o'er the o-cean In love's de-vo-tion O come to me.
Sure Ka-ty dar-ling, My heart is burning, My heart is yearning for bliss and for thee.
The Daisy.
JAMES MONTGOMERY.
Arr. by H. R. PALMER, by per.
1. There is a flower, a lit - tle flower, With sil - ver crest and
2. On waste and wood - land, rock, and plain, Its hum - ble buds un -
La la la la la la la la la la la la la la la la la la la
gold - en eye, That wel - comes eve - ry chang - ing hour. And
heed - ed rise: The rose has but a sum - mer reign, The
la la la la la la la la la la la la la la la la la la

weath - ers eve - ry sky............
dai - sy nev - er dies............
Fine.
la la la la la la la la la la.
La la la la la la
D. C.
la la la la la la la la la la la la la la la.
Good Morning.
Thos. Hastings, Mus. Dr.
Wm. B. Bradbury, by per.
pp
ff
f
1. This beau - ti - ful morn, so bright and clear, Smiles
2. The birds of the for - - est join in song, The
3. The moun - tain and hills are crowned with light, The
o - ver the lawn our hearts to cheer, Smiles o - ver the lawn our
flocks and the herds still graze a - long, The flocks and the herds still
sun is a - ris - ing clear and bright, The sun is a - ris - - ing
hearts to cheer. Good morn - ing, good morn - ing, good morn - ing.
graze a : long. Good morn - ing, good morn - ing, good morn - ing.
clear and bright. Good morn - ing, good morn - ing, good morn - ing.

118
Roaming.
Sprightly.
German.
1. Up and down, o'er hills and meads, Rid - ing, walk - ing, quick or slow,
2. Peo - ple good, and free, and kind, Meet my eye in ev - 'ry place;
3. Ne'er in lone - li - ness I pine, For I march to mu - sic free;
On, wher - ev - er fan - cy leads, O'er the fair, bright world I'll
Near the cheer-ful hearth and board, Still the wanderer finds a
Friend, if thou the song can join, Take thy staff and come with
go, Yes, yes, yes, yes, O'er the fair, bright world I'll go.
place, Yes, yes, yes, yes, Still the wan - derer finds a place.
me, Yes, yes, yes, yes, Take thy staff and come with me.
Blue Bells of Scotland.
Arr. H. P. M.
1. O where and O where is your High-land lad - die gone?
2. O where and O where did your High-land lad - die dwell?
3. Sup - pose and sup - pose that your High-land lad should die?
He's gone to fight the French, for King George up - on the throne--And it's
He dwelt in mer - ry Scot - land, At sign of the Blue Bell — And it's
The bag - pipes should play o'er him, And I'd sit down and cry — But it's

O in my heart, I wish him safe at home.
O in my heart, I love my lad - die well.
O in my heart, I hope he may not die.
Evening on the Lake. (Glee.)
H. H. Hayden.
M. L. Bartlett, by per.
1. Now brightly on the yield-ing wave, The moon's soft rays are glanc - ing, The
2. We gai - ly dip the gleaming oar, And on-ward now are dash - ing, While
spark-ling wa - ter seems to move, As if with joy 'twere danc - ing.
faint and faint - er grows the shore, On which the waves are plash - ing.
And we are full of answering glee, With hap - py hearts we sing, And
We bid each thought of sor - row flee, Care to the winds we fling, And
far a - cross the wa - ters free, Our mer - ry notes shall ring.

Sighing for Thee.

Fanny J. Crosby. Theodore E. Perkins.

Cantabile.
1. Sighing for thee, I am sighing for thee, Light of my soul in beauty
2. Sighing for thee, when the queen of the night, O - ver the world, her bright watch
3. O - ver the deep, like a bird to its nest,— O - ver the deep, while stars are
shin - ing; Ev - ery fond hope like the i - vy is twin - ing, Round the
keep - ing, Lulls me to rest, till, in dreams I am weep - ing, While thy
gleam - ing; Back to my home where the love-light is beam - ing, Glad - ly
heart that is dear-est to me:....
form like a vis - ion I see:....
now, I am fly - ing a - way:...
Con molto sentimento.
Sad was our part - ing, lone - ly I
Closely I fold thee, joy in my
Soon in thy beau - ty I shall be -
left thee, Oft I think of the promise we gave; When in the
bo - som Throbs a - new, as I call thee my own; Sor - row and
hold thee, Soon with joy wilt thou welcome me home; Then will I

Ritardando.
twi - light, pensively ten - der, All was still but the voice of the wave.
part - ing, fade in-to pleas - ure, Yet I wake, and the vis - ion has flown.
ev - er linger be-side thee, Nev-er more on the ocean to roam.
Chorus.
Tempo primo.
Sigh-ing for thee,...... I am sigh-ing for thee,........ Light of my
Sighing for thee, for thee I am sigh - ing,
soul in beau-ty shin - ing; Every fond hope...... like the i - vy is
Light of my soul in beauty now shin - ing; Every fond hope like
Rallentando.
twin - - ing, Round the heart...... that is dear-est to me........
Rit.
i - vy is twin - ing, Twining a - round the heart, dearest, to me.

The Sleigh-Ride.

T. F. Seward.
Arr. from Gottschalk, by T. F. Seward.
Sempre Marcato.
1. How bright and clear, The snow-beams sparkle far and near, With hearts so light, We
2. How swift we go, So lightly o'er the frosty snow, With friends beside, How
Jing-a-ling, jing-a-ling, Jing-a-ling, jing-a-ling,
greet this joy-ful night. Brilliant stars so brightly shining, Snow-drifts up the
mer - ri - ly we ride.
hill-sides climbing, Hoofs that dance with music's chiming, What a scene of gay de - light!
Jin - gle go the bells so mer-ri - ly, Hap - py hearts and fa - ces beaming,
Jing-a-ling, jing-a-ling, jing-a-ling, jing - a - ling,
Voi - ces sing - ing out so cheer - i - ly, What a joy - ful,
Jing - a - ling, jing - a - ling, jing - a - ling, jing - a - ling,

1st.
2d.
joy - ful night, joy - ful night! With hearts so
Jing - a - ling,
ff
light We greet this joy - ful night.
jing - a - ling, Jing - a - ling, jing - a - ling, jing, jing, jing.
Sleep, my Darling.
Arr. by Hubert P. Main, by per.
Slowly.
1. Sleep, my dar - ling, take thy rest; Pil - lowed on a moth - er's breast:
2. May their kind and fost - 'ring care Guard thy heart from ev - ery snare;
Slum - ber sweet - ly thro' the night, Slum - ber till the morn - ing light;
Oh, a - bove thy gen - tle head May their ra - diant wings be spread!
May good an - gels vig - il keep, While thine eyes are closed in sleep.
Sleep! my dar - ling, take thy rest, Pil - lowed on a moth - er's breast.

Jolly Boys.

Written and arr. by F. LE CLAIR. Arr. by H. R. PALMER, by per.

1. There is a school of jol - ly boys, You'll find them hard to beat;
2. They stud - y hard from nine till twelve, From one P. M. till four;

They al - ways have a right good time When - e'er they chance to meet.
But quick-ly gath - er on the green When stu - dy hours are o'er.

And they al - ways seem so jol - ly, oh! So jol - ly oh! So

jol - ly, oh! And they always seem so jol - ly, oh! Where-ev - er they may

be; They sing, they play, they laugh ha, ha, they laugh ha, ha, They sing, they

play, What jol - ly boys are they! Fal la la, fal la la, fal la, la, fal la la, fal la la, fal la la, fal de the ral de the

ral lal li do, Slap,* bang,* here they come again, here they come a-gain,

here they come again, Slap,* bang,* here they come again, What jol-ly boys are they.

* These two words should be accompanied by striking the hands together, or striking the desk with the fists.

Come, Soft and Lovely Evening.

Laur.
1. Come, soft and love-ly eve - ning, Spread o'er the grass - y fields;
2. See, where the clouds are weav-ing A rich and gol - den chain;
3. All na - ture now is si - lent, Ex - cept the pass - ing breeze;
4. Sweet eve - ning, thou art with us, So tran-quil, mild, and still;
We love the peace-ful feel - ing Thy si - lent com - ing yields.
See how the dark-ened shad - ow Ex - tends a - long the plain.
And birds, their night-song warb - ling A - mong the dew - y trees.
Thou dost our thank-ful bos - oms With hum - ble prais - es fill.

Home, Dear Home.

FANNY J. CROSBY.
THEODORE E. PERKINS, by per.
1. I come, I come with a bound-ing heart, A - cross the heav - ing sea; A
2. A cot - tage nest - ling in the vale, Of ros - es sweet and fair; The
3. A fa - ther's pray'r, a moth - er's tear, A sis - ter's warm ca - ress, A
wand-'rer from a dis - tant clime. My na - tive land, to thee;
rob - in and his leaf - y nest, The brooklet, all are there;
broth-er's wel - come, all com - bine This hallowed hour to bless;
Proud-ly I watch thy glow-ing skies, Be - neath whose a - zure dome, I
Glad - ly I see the broad green hills Where boyhood loved to roam, My
What are the fest - ive halls of mirth, That lure us while we roam, To
feel a - gain the hal - lowed dream Of home, dear home.
lips are mute, I on - ly feel 'Tis home, dear home.
one kind look from those we love At home, dear home.

Cradle Song.
THEODORE F. SEWARD, by per.
1. Sleep, ba - by, sleep! Thy fa - ther watch-es the sheep; Thy mother is shaking the dream-land tree, And down falls a lit - tle dream on thee; Sleep, baby, sleep! Sleep, ba - by, sleep!
2. Sleep, ba - by, sleep! The large stars are the sheep; The lit - tle stars are the lambs, I guess, The fair moon is the shep - herd-ess; &c.
3. Sleep, ba - by, sleep! And cry not like a sheep; Else will the sheep - dog bark and whine, And bite this naught-y child of mine; &c.
4. Sleep, ba - by, sleep! A - way! and tend the sheep; A - way, thou black dog, fierce and wild, And do not wake my lit - tle child! &c.
Rit.
The Bell doth Toll. (Round.)
The bell doth toll, I love its roll, Its song I know full well;
I love its ring - ing, For it calls to sing - ing, With its bim bim bim bome bell, Bim, bim, bim bim bim bome bell.
Morning Bells. (Round.)
Morning bells I love to hear, Ring-ing mer-ri - ly, loud and clear.

Sweet Summer Time.

Arr. by Edward A. Perkins.
1. Oh! the sweet Summer time for me, for me, When we dance, and we sing so light and free; When the birds gai - ly car - ol thro' the air, And the leaves are so green, so fresh and fair.
2. Thro' the val - ley runs the murm - 'ring stream, And the war - bler's song comes from the shade; All na - ture charms with bright - est beams, And all things seem for glad - ness made.
3. Let oth - ers sing for the Win - ter king, Let them give loud shouts for the mer - ry Spring, But a - loud each voice shall sing in praise Of the bright and the sun - ny sum - mer days.
Then sing a song for the bright summer time,
Sweet Summer, gay Summer, bright Summer time,
Sing a song for the bright Summer time.
Sweet Summer, gay Summer,

From *Western Bell* by permission of O. Ditson & Co

.... Tra la la la la la la la la la la la la

bright Summer time.

la la la la la la la la la la la la la la la la la la la

la la la la la la la la la la la

la la la la la la la la la la la la la la la la la.

Old John Cross. (Round.)

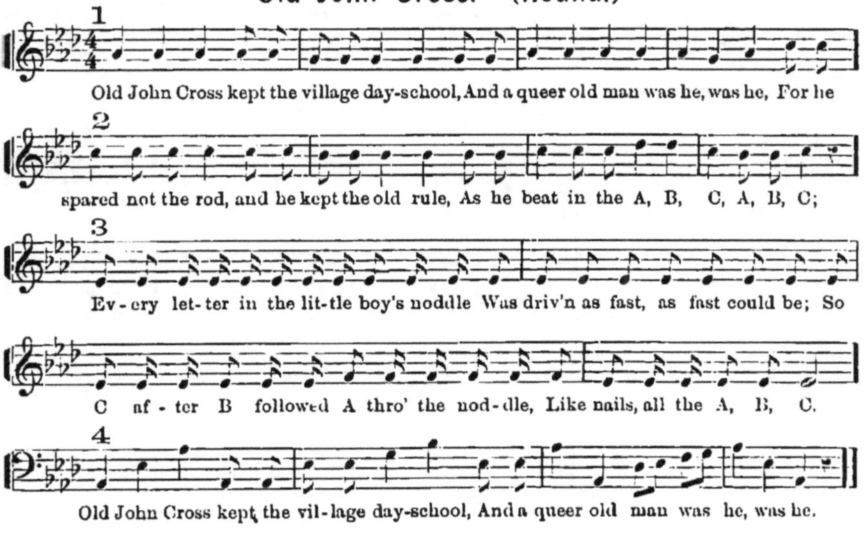

1

Old John Cross kept the village day-school, And a queer old man was he, was he, For he

2

spared not the rod, and he kept the old rule, As he beat in the A, B, C, A, B, C;

3

Ev - ery let- ter in the lit-tle boy's noddle Was driv'n as fast, as fast could be; So

C af - ter B followed A thro' the nod-dle, Like nails, all the A, B, C.

4

Old John Cross kept the vil-lage day-school, And a queer old man was he, was he.

The Last Rose of Summer.

Arr. by Hubert P. Main.
1. 'Tis the last rose of summer, Left bloom-ing a - lone, All her love-ly
2. I'll not leave thee, thou lone one, To pine on the stem; Since the love-ly
3. So soon may I follow, When friendships de - cay; And from love's shin-
com - panions Are fad - ed and gone; No flower of her kindred, No
are sleeping, So sleep thou with them; Thus, kindly I scatter Thy
ing cir - cle The gems drop a - way! When true hearts are withered, And
Ritard.
rose-bud is nigh To re - flect back her blushes, Or give sigh for sigh.
leaves o'er thy bed, Where thy mates of the garden Lie scentless and dead.
fond ones are flown, Oh! who would in - hab - it This bleak world a - lone?
Those Evening Bells. (Round.)
1
Those evening bells, those evening bells, How many a tale their mu - sic tells,
2
Of youth, and home, and that sweet time When first we heard their soothing chime;
3
Those ringing, jingling, evening bells, How many a tale their mu - sic tells:
4

Those evening bells, those evening bells, How many a tale their mu - sic tells.

Home, Sweet Home.

John Howard Payne, 1821.
Arr. by H. P. M.
1. Mid pleasures and pal - a - ces, though we may roam, Be it ev - er so humble, there's no place like home; A charm from the skies seems to hal - low us there, Which, seek thro' the world, is ne'er met with else - where. Home!
2. An ex - ile from home, splen-dor daz - zles in vain; O! give me my low - ly thatched cottage a - gain, — The birds sing-ing gai - ly, that came at my call; Give me them, with the peace of mind, dear - er than all.
Cres.
Rit.
Cres.
home! sweet, sweet home! Be it ev - er so humble, there's no place like home.
He who would Lead a Happy Life. (Round.)
1
2
3
He who would lead a hap - py life, He who would lead a hap - py life, Must keep himself from an - gry strife, Must keep him - self from an - gry strife.

Somebody's Coming.

From The Cantata of "SANTA CLAUS." W. H. DOANE, by per.

Andante con espressione.

p Dolce.

1. I have a se - cret, 'tis ev - er so bright, How it will please you, a -
2. He is no stranger, this ver - y old man, All of you know him; but
3. May be he'll bring you a bun-dle of toys, Nice lit - tle pres - ents for

muse and de - light, Yes, a new pleas-ure is now on its way,
guess, if you can, Why he is com - ing, and what he will say,
girls and for boys, Some-bod - y's com - ing who loves you right well,

One you'll re - member for ma - ny a day. Some - bod - y's com-ing, and
Hundred of miles he has journey'd to-day.
How you would laugh if his name I should tell.

who can it be? Some-bod - y's com-ing, but wait till you see.
Some-bod-y's com-ing and who can it be? Some-bod - y's com-ing but
Rall.
wait till you see.
f Rall.
ff
Now the Day is Gone. (Round.)
1
2
Now the day is gone, And the night is come, When the
3
4
day of life is flown, May heav'n be our home.

Swinging 'Neath the Old Apple Tree.

Words and Music by Oren R. Barrows, by per.
Moderato.
1. Oh, the sports of child-hood! Roaming thro' the wild-wood, Run - ning o'er the
2. Sway-ing in the sun - beams, Float-ing in the shad - ow, Sail - ing on the
meadows, hap - py and free; But my heart's a beat - ing For the old - time
breez - es, hap - py and free; Chas-ing all our sad - ness, Shout ing in our
greet - ing, Swinging 'neath the old ap - ple - tree.
glad - ness, Swinging 'neath the old ap - ple - tree.
Chorus.
Swing - ing, swing - ing,
Swing - - ing,
Swing - ing, swing - ing, Lull - ing care to rest 'neath the old ap - ple tree,
Swing - - ing, Swing - ing 'neath the old ap - ple tree,
Swinging, swinging, Swinging, swinging, Swinging 'neath the old ap - ple - tree.
Swing - - ing, Swing - - ing,

Under the Snow Drops.

T. H. Edson.
Theodore E. Perkins, by per.
Andante.
1. Un - der the snow drops rest two lit-tle
2. Two lit - tle hands on a calm cold
3. Un - der the snow drops a grave is
feet, Un - der the snow drops two blue eyes sleep; Part - ed a - way from the
breast Are fold -ed a - way, for ev - er at rest; Two sweet lips will be
made, Un - der the snow drops my treasure is laid; Un - der the snow drops, it
fore - head fair Lies ma - ny a wave of soft brown hair.
part-ed no more Till they sweet - ly sing on the shin - - ing shore.
can - not be; I'm sure that in heaven my child waits for me.

136 O Songs of the Beautiful.

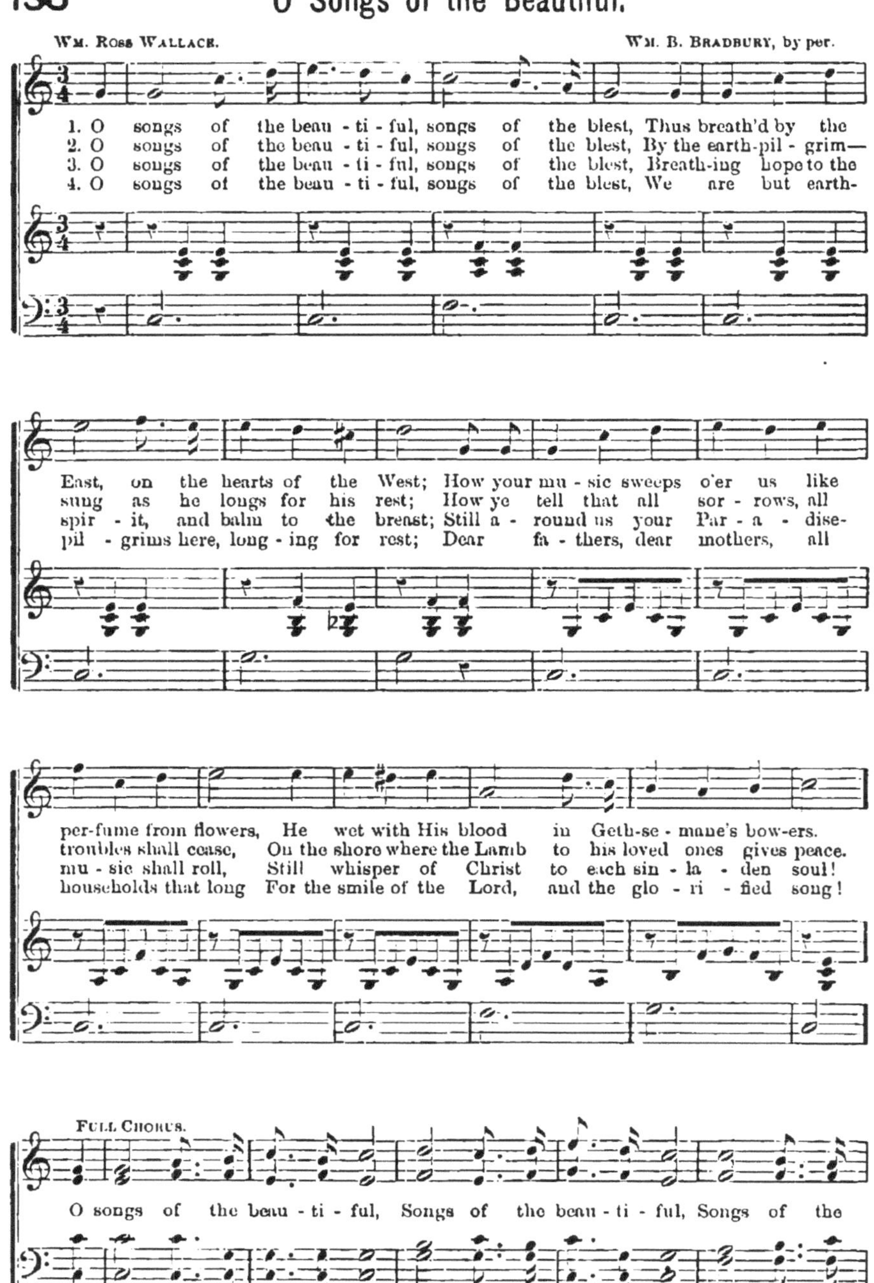
Wm. Ross Wallace.
Wm. B. Bradbury, by per.
1. O songs of the beau - ti - ful, songs of the blest, Thus breath'd by the
2. O songs of the beau - ti - ful, songs of the blest, By the earth-pil - grim—
3. O songs of the beau - ti - ful, songs of the blest, Breath-ing hope to the
4. O songs of the beau - ti - ful, songs of the blest, We are but earth-
East, on the hearts of the West; How your mu - sic sweeps o'er us like
sung as he longs for his rest; How ye tell that all sor - rows, all
spir - it, and balm to the breast; Still a - round us your Par - a - dise-
pil - grims here, long - ing for rest; Dear fa - thers, dear mothers, all
per-fume from flowers, He wet with His blood in Geth-se - mane's bow-ers.
troubles shall cease, On the shore where the Lamb to his loved ones gives peace.
mu - sic shall roll, Still whisper of Christ to each sin - la - den soul!
households that long For the smile of the Lord, and the glo - ri - fied song!
Full Chorus.
O songs of the beau - ti - ful, Songs of the beau - ti - ful, Songs of the

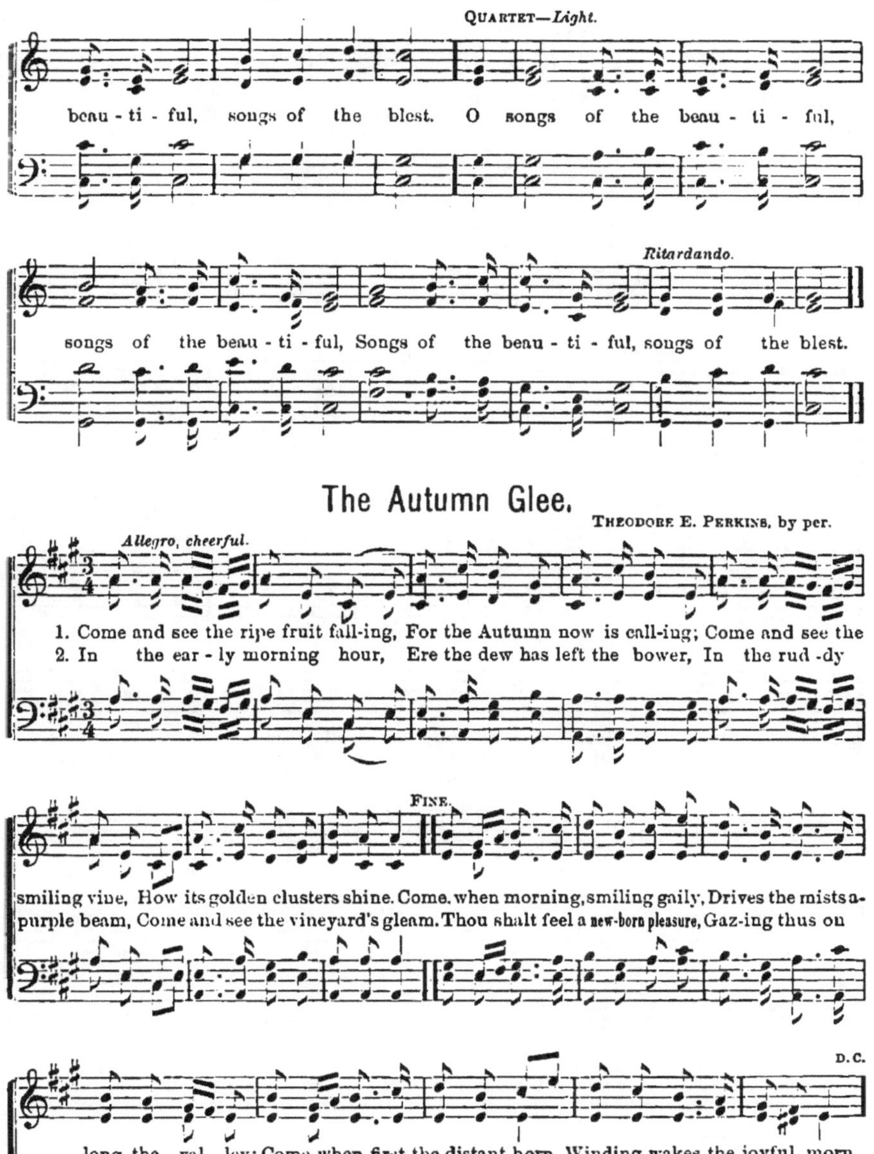
QUARTET—Light.
beau - ti - ful, songs of the blest. O songs of the beau - ti - ful,
Ritardando.
songs of the beau - ti - ful, Songs of the beau - ti - ful, songs of the blest.
The Autumn Glee.
THEODORE E. PERKINS, by per.
Allegro, cheerful.
1. Come and see the ripe fruit fall-ing, For the Autumn now is call-ing; Come and see the
2. In the ear - ly morning hour, Ere the dew has left the bower, In the rud -dy
FINE.
smiling vine, How its golden clusters shine. Come, when morning, smiling gaily, Drives the mists a-
purple beam, Come and see the vineyard's gleam. Thou shalt feel a new-born pleasure, Gaz-ing thus on
D. C.
long the val - ley; Come, when first the distant horn Winding wakes the joyful morn.
Autumn's treasure, And the joy-ful songs shall raise, Sweet-er notes of grateful praise.

Killarney.

M. W. BALFE.

Moderato.
1. By Kil-lar - ney's lakes and fells, Em - 'rald isles and winding bays,
2. No place else can charm the eye With such bright and va - ried tints,
3. Mu - sic there for ech - o dwells, Makes each sound a har - mo - ny,
pp
Moun - tain paths and woodland dells, Mem - 'ry ev - er fond - ly strays;
Ev - 'ry rock that you pass by, Ver - dure broid - ers or besprints,
Ma - ny voiced the cho - rus swells, 'Till it faints in ec - sta - cy;
Boun - teous na - ture loves all lands, Beau - ty wanders
Vir - gin there the green grass grows, Ev - 'ry morn springs
With the charmful tints be - low, Seems the Heav'n a -
Cres.
rf
pp
ev - 'ry where, Foot-prints leaves on ma - ny strands, But her home is
na - tal day, Bright hued ber - ries daff the snows, Smil - ing win - ter's
bove to vie, All rich col - ors that we know, Ting the cloud-wreaths
Colla parte.

Dim. pp a tempo.
sure - ly there! An - gels fold their wings and rest, In that E - den
frown a - way. An - gels oft - en pass - ing there, Doubt if E - den
in that sky. Wings of an - gels so might shine, Glanc - ing back soft
Rit. pp a tempo.
Cres.
f
of the west, Beau - ty's home Kil - lar - ney, Ev - er fair Kil - lar - ney.
were more fair, Beau - ty's home Kil - lar - ney, Ev - er fair Kil - lar - ney.
light di - vine, Beau - ty's home Kil - lar - ney, Ev - er fair Kil - lar - ney.
f
A, B, C, Song.
FRANK FOREST.
AUGUST POHLENZ, arr. by H. R. P., by per.
1. A, B, C, D, Come sing with me, Sing we this pleas - ant song,
2. H, I, J, K, This is the way, Sing we so mer - ri - ly,
3. Q, R, S, T, Eas - y you see, For when we all a - gree,
It is not ver - y long, B, C, D, E, F, G, Come sing with me.
Blithely and cheer - i - ly, K, L, M, N, O, P, Come sing with me.
Stud - y will light - er be, T, U, V, W, X, Y & Z.

Farewell, Dear Home.

MARY C. SEWARD.
ARR. from FELICIEN DAVID, by T. F. S., by per.
Affettuoso.
1. Farewell, dear home, farewell! I now must leave thee, With all thy pleasant scenes I
2. Farewell, dear home, farewell! with bosom yearning, To lin - ger still with dear ones
now must part; Farewell, dear friends, farewell! tho' deep it grieve me, While fondest mem'ries
fold - ed here; Farewell, dear friends, farewell! tho' hearts are burning, With love that absence
linger on my heart, farewell! Wherev-er I may wander, wherev - er I roam, My
on-ly makes more dear, farewell! In foreign lands a stranger, tho' lone-ly I roam, To
My home, dear home!
tho'ts shall still be with thee, My home, dear home!
thee my heart returning, My home, dear home!
How I can leave thee, Home of my childhood,
Tho'ts so endearing, Comforting, cheering,
1st.
2d.
Where the true and loving meet, With love to greet.
Happy fa-ces, loving (Omit. . . . .)
hearts, All, all, farewell! Farewell, dear home, fare-

Dear home, fare-
well, I now must leave thee, With all thy pleasant scenes I now must part.
well, ... Dear home, farewell, ...
Home, dear home, farewell, Home, dear home, farewell, Fare-well, fare - well !
Autumn is Sighing Around Me.
Fanny J. Crosby.
Theodore E. Perkins, by per.
Con espressione.
1. Au - tumn is sigh - ing a - round me, Tell - ing a tale of the
2. Light and its sun-shine is fad - ing, Soon will its ros - es de -
past, Fold - ing the leaves on her bo - som, With - ered and
cay; All the sweet buds I have cher - ished, Fade like the
With-ered and chill'd in the blast.
Ritard
chill'd in the blast, With-ered and chill'd in the blast.
sum - mer a - way, Fade like the sum - mer a - way.

My Ain Sailor Laddie.

George Cooper. Hubert P. Main.

p
1. Oh, my poor heart is breaking, Sae sad is its ach - ing! "The
2. Oh, the sad hours were drear - y, And storms nev - er wea - ry: No
3. Oh, the long days were wan - ing, And chill winds com-plain-ing; Yet
sweet las - sie whispered," "oh, stay!" But her lad - die, so lov - ing, A -
word to the las - sie e'er came, For her lad - die she wait - ed, And
joy to the las - sie came not; For her lad - die, so lov - ing, A -
far must be rov - ing: He kissed her bright tears a - way; Tho'
spring birds were mat-ed While lone - ly she breathed his name; But
far was still rov - ing, By all, save her - self, for - got; But

seas may sev - er, be mine for - ev - er! And I
ne'er for - get - ting, though suns were set - ting, And an -
pain and sor - row bring joy to - mor - row, And the
prom-ise for aye to be true!" Then her lad - die, sore - hearted, in
oth - er came fondly to woo, For her lad - die still weep-ing, her
lad - die soon learned this was true, For her lad - die back roam-ing she
si - lence de - part - ed, Where bil - lows were roll - ing so blue.
watch she was keep - ing Where bil - lows were roll - ing so blue.
clasped in the gloam-ing, Where bil - lows were roll - ing so blue.

Chorus.
Oh, lad - die sae lov - ing! Oh, lad - die far rov - ing! Aye,
bon - nie as bon - nie can be! For my lad - die I'm sing - ing, And
white sails I'm bring - ing My ain sail - or lad - die for me.

Evening Song.
TRIO.
Franz Abt.
Andante sostenuto. pp
1. The evening bells sound clearly, They call the vale to rest; Around fall night's soft stillness, The
2. The moon roves softly, gliding Her heavenly path a-long; The plan- ets pass her greeting, But
But
sun sinks in the west; A ho - ly silence keeping, The stars watch nature sleeping, She's
hush-ed is their song; And as to seraph numbers, Be - low the sweet earth slumbers, She's
hush-ed is their song; And as to ser - aph
p
ff
pp
come in soft red light, She's come in soft red light, The qui - et night, the qui - et night!
come, &c.
O Sing with Voices Clear Strong.
TRIO.
Methfessel.
Allegretto.
1. O sing with voic - es clear and strong, The song of songs up - rais - ing; Our
2. Thou old - en, bar - dic fa - ther-land, Thou land of truth and beau - ty, Thou
3. With thee for aye we cast our lot; To home and vir - tue tru - ly We
own, our fa - ther's na - tive song, Set wood-land ech - oes prais - ing.
dear, thou well be - lov - ed land, Thy praise is joy and du - ty.
ded - i - cate our hand, and heart, And soul, and spir - it new - ly.

146 The Merry Harvest Moon.

FANNY J. CROSBY.
THEODORE E. PERKINS, by per.
Spirited.
1. The mer - ry har-vest moon is beam - ing, So brightly o'er the yel - low grain,
2. Oh, wel - come har-vest time, we hail thee, And trip a - way in spor - tive glee,
That, grace-ful in its light is wav - ing In beau - ty o'er the dew - y
While star - ry eyes are fond - ly smil - ing, And zeph-yrs mur - mur light and
A - way, a - way,
ff
Staccato.
plain; A - way, a - way, we love with the young and
free, A - way, &c.
And dance, And dance,
gay to roam, And dance, and dance by the light of the har - vest
moon. See the lit - tle dai - sies as we pass, Hid - ing, hid - ing in the

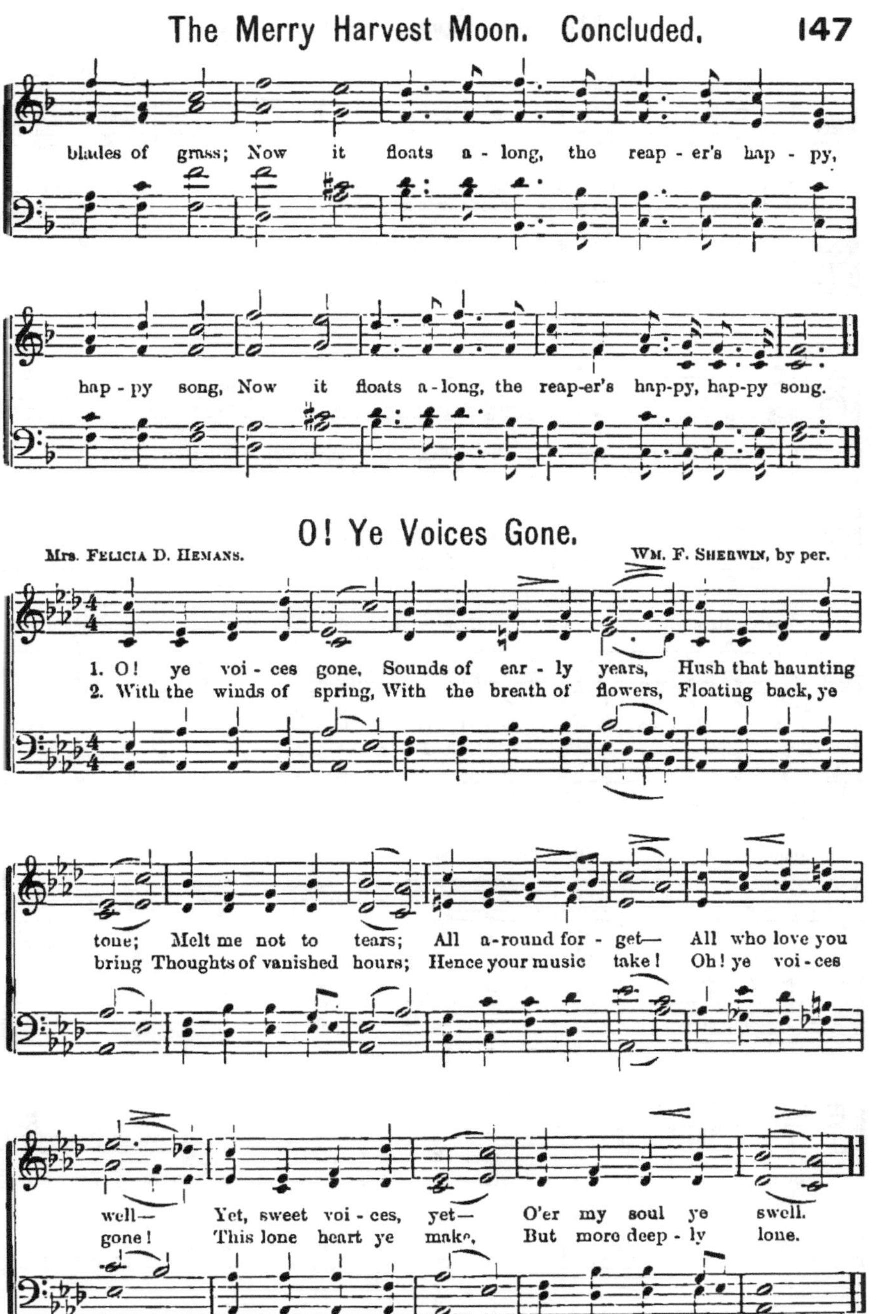
blades of grass; Now it floats a - long, the reap - er's hap - py,
hap - py song, Now it floats a - long, the reap-er's hap-py, hap-py song.
O! Ye Voices Gone.
Mrs. Felicia D. Hemans.
Wm. F. Sherwin, by per.
1. O! ye voi - ces gone, Sounds of ear - ly years, Hush that haunting
2. With the winds of spring, With the breath of flowers, Floating back, ye
tone; Melt me not to tears; All a-round for - get— All who love you
bring Thoughts of vanished hours; Hence your music take! Oh! ye voi - ces
well— Yet, sweet voi - ces, yet— O'er my soul ye swell.
gone! This lone heart ye make, But more deep - ly lone.

In My Own Sweet Native Vale.

Alex. Lee.

Allegretto. p
1. I would not be a fai - ry light, To dance on moonbeam's ray,
2. For there the mountain maidens meet Their swains with lov - ing song;
Cres.
I would not be an el - fin sprite, To shun the glo-rious day;
And fai - ries lead, with un - seen feet, Their moon-light dance a - long:
My
p heart still sighs for cloudless skies, I love the perfumed
pp
La la la la la la la la la la la la la la la la la la
pp
gale, Oh! let me be a blue-bell free,
Cres.
la la la la la la la la la la la la la la la la la
In my
own sweet na - tive vale, In my own.... sweet na - tive vale, In my
la,
p

own.................. sweet vale, In my own...... sweet
na - tive vale, In my own sweet na - - tive vale.
f
My Dog Dash.
Theodore E. Perkins, by per.
1. My dog Dash is full of fun, Bow, wow, wow, wow, wow; See him jump, and
2. Now he's romping far a - way, Bow, wow, wow, wow, wow; Now he's roll - ing
roll, and run, Bow, wow, wow, wow, wow; Lis-ten to his joy-ful bark, Bow, wow,
in the hay, Bow, wow, wow, wow, wow; Bet-ter dog you ne'er did see, Bow, wow,
wow, wow, wow; As he scampers through the park, Bow, wow, wow, wow, wow.
wow, wow, wow; I love "Dash" and "Dash" loves me, Bow, wow, wow, wow, wow.

The Bird Carol.

WM. B. BRADBURY, by per.

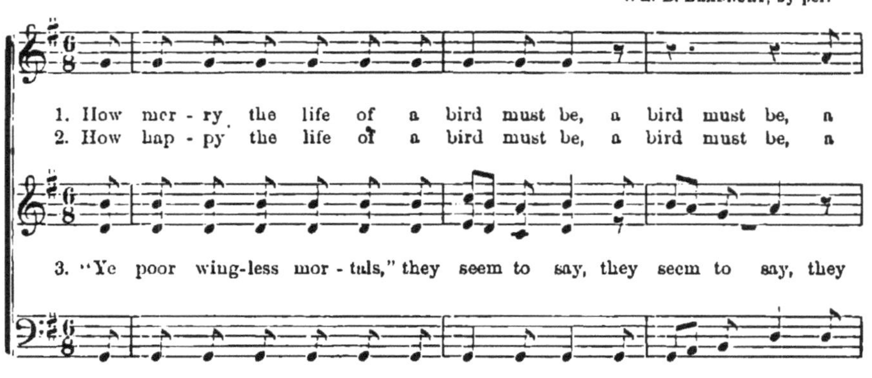
1. How mer - ry the life of a bird must be, a bird must be, a
2. How hap - py the life of a bird must be, a bird must be, a
3. "Ye poor wing-less mor - tals," they seem to say, they seem to say, they

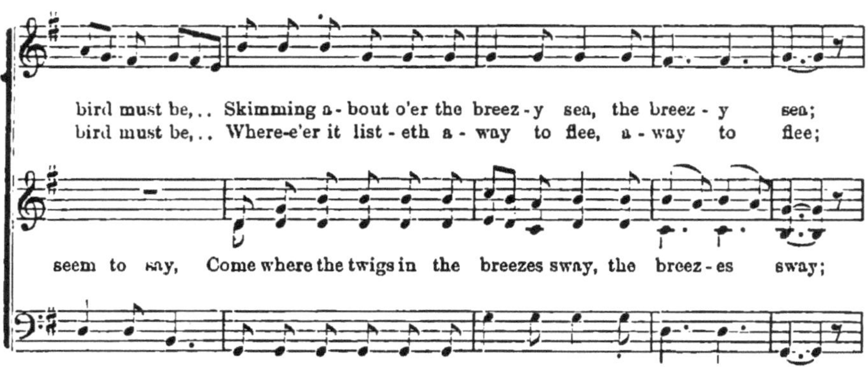
bird must be, . . Skimming a - bout o'er the breez - y sea, the breez - y sea;
bird must be, . . Where-e'er it list - eth a - way to flee, a - way to flee;
seem to say, Come where the twigs in the breezes sway, the breez - es sway;

Crest - ing the bil - lows like sil - ver - y foam, And wheel - ing a -
Sail - ing where-ev - er its fan - cy may call, Then dash - ing a -
Sing - ing and swing - ing, the world here is fair, The leaves are all

WHISTLING DUET.
way to its cliff - built home.
down thro' the wa - ter - fall.
Whistle or Flute.
danc - ing in soft summer air.
Accomp.—Vocal or Inst.
Jack and Gill.
H. L. HANDY, by per.
1. Jack and Gill went up the hill, To draw a pail of wa - ter,
2. Lit - tle Jane ran up the lane, To hang her clothes a dry - ing,
3. Nim - ble Dick ran up so quick, He tumbled o - ver a tim - ber,
4. Care - ful Mat took up the cat, And flung her in the wa - ter,
5. Whined one young pike, "I do not like A cat here in the riv - er,"
6. Here came a trout, and flounced a - bout, And made his gills to rat - tle,
7. 'Twas pike and trout, now in, now out, Till when they both went un - der,
8. And all this ill, when Jack and Gill, Went for that pail of wa - ter,
Jack fell down and broke his crown, And Gill came tumbling af - ter.
She called for Nell to ring the bell, For Jack and Gill were dy - ing.
He bent his bow to shoot a crow, And killed poor puss in the win - dow.
The fish - es 'round came at the sound, To see what made the splatter.
"Hush! hush! she's dead," an old pike said, And I will eat her liv - er."
"Leave her for me a - lone," cried he; And then there came a bat - tle.
An eel slipped in as sly as sin, And car - ried off the plunder.
And Jack fell down and broke his crown, And Gill came tumbling af - ter.

152 On Alpine Heights.

German

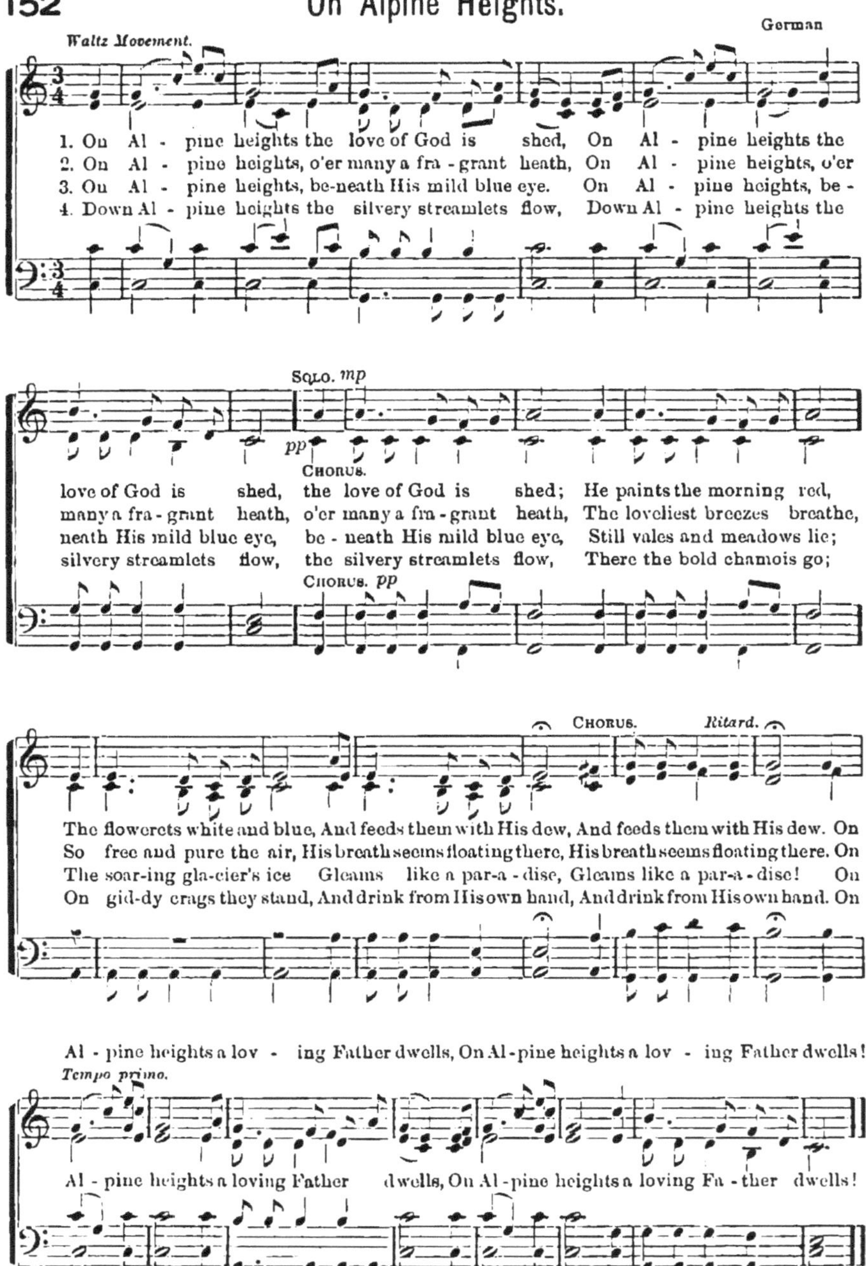
Waltz Movement.
1. On Al - pine heights the love of God is shed, On Al - pine heights the love of God is shed, the love of God is shed; He paints the morning red,
2. On Al - pine heights, o'er many a fra - grant heath, On Al - pine heights, o'er many a fra - grant heath, o'er many a fra - grant heath, The loveliest breezes breathe,
3. On Al - pine heights, be-neath His mild blue eye. On Al - pine heights, be - neath His mild blue eye, be - neath His mild blue eye, Still vales and meadows lie;
4. Down Al - pine heights the silvery streamlets flow, Down Al - pine heights the silvery streamlets flow, the silvery streamlets flow, There the bold chamois go;
Solo. mp
pp
Chorus.
Chorus. pp
The flowerets white and blue, And feeds them with His dew, And feeds them with His dew. On
So free and pure the air, His breath seems floating there, His breath seems floating there. On
The soar-ing gla-cier's ice Gleams like a par-a - dise, Gleams like a par-a - dise! On
On gid-dy crags they stand, And drink from His own hand, And drink from His own hand. On
Chorus.
Ritard.
Al - pine heights a lov - ing Father dwells, On Al - pine heights a lov - ing Father dwells!
Tempo primo.
Al - pine heights a loving Father dwells, On Al - pine heights a loving Fa - ther dwells!
Al - pine heights a lov - ing Father dwells!

Now the Moon is Gleaming.

F. J. C. — THEODORE E. PERKINS, by per.

Allegro.
1. Now the moon is gleam-ing, O'er the wa-ters beam-ing, Mel-low light,
Fai-ry sprites are danc-ing, Love-lit eyes are glanc-ing, Wel-come hour,
2. Still the moon is smil-ing, Ev-ery thought beguil-ing, Sum-mer moon,
Who would think of sor-row, Leave it till to-mor-row, Wel-come hour,
1st.
2d.
FINE.
Soft-ly bright, O'er the earth she throws;
(Omit.................................)
Mag-ic hour of sweet re-pose.
Playful moon, Lovely queen of night;
(Omit.................................)
Tranquil hour of gay de-light.
O'er the lil-y sleep-ing, Pearl-y dews are weep-ing, While the moon,
Dis-tant bells are peal-ing, O'er the bil-low steal-ing, As we glide,
Laughing moon, Steals the drops so gen-tly fall-ing; Thus while na-ture slum-bers,
O'er the tide, Still the gen-tle sound is floating; I-dle winds are sigh-ing,
p Cres - cen - do.
ff
D. C. 1st Verse.
May our tuneful num-bers O'er some dreaming heart we prize In air-y vis-ions rise.
Rus-tic vales re-ply-ing, Hail the golden harvest moon That shines so bright and fair.

Raindrop Chorus.

R. S. TAYLOR. WM. B. BRADBURY, by per.

pp and gentle; staccato, in imitation of gentle raindrops.
f
1. When down the hills, The lit - tle rills No more in glee are flow - ing,
2. When ev - ery flower, In field and bower, Is drooping low and dy - ing,
pp
And fierce-ly down, With burn-ing frown The sum - mer sun is glow - ing;
When songs of birds, No more are heard, Each with the oth - er vie - ing,
ff
'Tis then with joy we greet the gales That waft us clouds with snowy sails, From
'Tis then with joy we greet the gales That waft us clouds with snowy sails, O'er
1st time p, 2d time f and joyfully.
dis - tant re-gions blowing, From distant re-gions blowing. Tat, tat, tat, tat, tat,
hill and val - ley fly - ing, O'er hill and val - ley fly - ing. Fall soft - ly o'er the
tat, tat, tat, tat, tat, tat, tat, tat, tat, tat, tat. Pat-ter, pat-ter, pat-ter,
thirst-y earth, O gen - tle sum - mer rain, Till grain - clad
Tat, tat, tat, Pat-ter, pat-ter, pat-ter,

Cres.
In the repeat the Tenor and Soprano may change parts.
pat-ter, pat-ter, pat-ter, pat-ter, pat-ter, In beau-ty smile a-gain.
hills and fer-tile vales,
pat-ter, pat-ter, pat-ter, pat-ter, pat-ter.
Twilight is Stealing.
Aldine S. Kieffer.
B. C. Unseld, by per.
1. Twi-light is steal-ing O-ver the sea, Shadows are fall-ing Dark on the lea;
2. Voi-ces of loved ones! Songs of the past! Still lin-ger round me, While life shall last
3. Come in the twi-light, Come, come to me! Bringing some message, O-ver the sea;
Borne on the night winds, Voi-ces of yore, Come from the far-off shore.
Lone-ly I wan-der, Sad-ly I roam, Seek-ing that far-off home.
Cheer-ing my path-way While here I roam, Seek-ing that far-off home.
Chorus.
Far a-way be-yond the star-lit skies, Where the love-light nev-er, nev-er dies
Gleameth a man-sion filled with de-light, Sweet hap-py home, so bright.

156

Good Night, Dear Friends.

Fanny J. Crosby. Theodore E. Perkins, by per.

Gay Little Dandelion.

B. C. Unseld, by per.

1. Good night, dear friends, the bell of time Is peal - ing now its sil - ver chime;
2. Good night, dear friends, the hallowed beam That clusters round this tran - quil scene,
3. Good night, dear friends, our parting lay, When oth - er years have passed a - way,
How sweet the ech - oes fall! An - oth - er hap - py eve is passed,
From sun - ny re - gions fall; We joy to catch their wel - come ray,
Will mem-'ry still re - call; May guard - ian an - gels gent - ly keep
Our part - ing hour has come at last, Good night, good night to all.
And still we lin - ger while we say, Good night to all.
Their vig - ils o'er your balm - y sleep, Good night, good night to all.
1. Gay lit - tle Dan - de-lion, lights up the meads, Swings on her slen - der foot
2. Cold lie the dai - sy banks clad but in green, Where in the May's a - gone
3. Brave lit - tle Dan - de-lion, fast falls the snow, Bend - ing the daf - fo - dills
tell - eth her beads; Lists to the rob - in's note poured from a - bove,
bright hues were seen; Wild pinks are slumbering, vi - o - lets de - lay,
haught-y head low; Un - der the flee - cy tent, care - less of cold,

Wise lit - tle Dan - de - lion cares not for love. Gay lit - tle Dan - de - lion,
True lit - tle Dan - de - lion greet - eth the way. Gay lit - tle, &c.
Blithe lit - tle Dan - de - lion count - eth her gold. Gay lit - tle, &c.
lights up the meads, Swings on her slen - der foot, tell - eth her beads.
Joy! Joy! now we are Free.
From the German.
1. Joy! joy! now we are free, Va - ca - tion time has come; We
2. Come, come, let us a - way, To those we love so dear; At
3. Wake, wake up with the dawn, And roam the fields so gay; Our
lay a - side our books with care, And haste the wel - come
home with friends we soon shall be, And part - ed ones we
hearts are bound-ing with de - light, The sum - mer days are
smile to share Of na - ture's woodland, ring - ing With sing - ing.
long to see, With joy will gath - er near us, And cheer us.
long and bright; The for - est glades are ring - ing With sing - ing.

158
When Mary was a Lassie.
T. A. N.
Hubert P. Main, by per.
1. The maple trees are tinged with red, The birch with golden yellow; And high above the orchard wall, Hang apples rich and mel - low; And that's the way thro' yon - der lane That looks so still and grassy, The way I took one Sunday eve, When Mary was a Lassie.
2. You'd hardly think that patient face, That looks so pale and faded, Was once the ver-y sweetest one, That ev-er bon - net shad-ed; But when I went thro' yon - der lane That looks so still and grassy, Those eyes were bright, those cheeks were fair, Then Mary was a Lassie.
3. Now on her face, though once so fair, We trace the deep'ning furrows, That many a weary care has worn, And many ten - der sor - rows; Four times to yonder church-yard, Thro' the lane so still and grassy, We've borne and laid a - way our dead, Since Mary was a Lassie.
4. And so you see I've grown to love The wrinkles more than roses; Earth's winter flow'rs are sweeter far Than all spring's dew-y po - sies; They'll car - ry us thro' yon - der lane That looks so still and grassy, A - down the lane I used to go, When Mary was a Lassie.

CHORUS.
When Ma - ry was a Las - sie, When Ma - ry was a Las - sie, Those
eyes were bright, those cheeks were fair, When Ma - ry was a Las - sie.
Rit.
Over the Hill the Daylight is Dying.
MARDELLA.
THEODORE E. PERKINS, by per.
1. O - ver the hill the day-light is dy - ing, O - ver the dell the soft wind is
2. O - ver the heart our childhood is dy - ing, O - ver the past our mem'ry is
sigh - ing, O - ver the greenwood grace-ful and light, The fair - ies are
sigh - ing; Morning of pleas-ure speeding thy flight, Ah, soon we shall
ten - der - ly breathing good night; Shadows creep on, shadows creep on.
bid thee a part - ing good night; Shadows creep on, shadows creep on.

160
Verdant Fields.
F. Silcher.
p Moderato.
Verdant fields, vio - lets blue, Cuck - oo calling,
p
Verdant fields, violets blue, Cuckoo calling,
Black - bird's song, sun - ny show - ers, Zeph - yrs soft.
Blackbird's song, Sun - ny show - ers, Zeph - yrs soft.
mf
When I hear such words of gladness, Chasing far all gloom and sadness, I must praise thee,
love - ly Spring, I must praise thee, love - ly Spring: When I hear such words of
f
gladness, Chas - ing far all gloom and sadness, I must praise thee, love - ly

Verdant Fields. Concluded.

Spring, I must praise thee, love-ly Spring, Love - ly Spring, Love-ly Spring.

Hark! What Mystic Sounds.

G. Verdi.

Tempo di Marcia.

1. Hark! what mys - tic sounds are these, Steal - ing soft - ly o'er the seas?
Whence that mu - sic soft and low, Sound - ing as the bil - lows flow?

2. List a - gain, the sound draws near, Fall - ing sweet-ly on the ear;
Borne up - on the breeze a - long, 'Tis the mermaid's eve - ning song.

Solo.*

'Tis...... the mermaid's song, Borne up - on....... the breeze a - long.

'Tis the mermaid's evening song, Borne up-on, up-on the breeze a - long.

* *The first strain may be sung with the second, in the repeat, if without the accompaniment.*

Let the Hills Resound with Song!

L. H. F. Du Terreaux. | Brinley Richards.

Molto animato.

f

Let the hills re-sound with song, As we proud-ly march a - long, For,

as of old, our sires were bold, Stout hearts have we; While Cambria's mountains

stand Like the ram-parts of the land, Un-fet-ter'd as the winds are her

chil-dren free. *ff* War we wage for free-dom's her - it - age, Our

cause is true that urg - es to the con-flict's close, *p* And peace shall crown, The

warrior's bright re-nown, The fame of him who bore him well in front of foes. Let the
hills re-sound with song, As we proudly march a - long, For, as of old our
sires were bold, Stout hearts have we; While Cambria's mountains stand Like the
rmmparts of the land, Un-fet - ter'd as the winds are her chil - dren free.
Land of my home, Tender thoughts will come,
p
Cres.
pp Land of home, my land of home, my land of home, my

Let the Hills Resound with Song! Continued.

When thy hap-py val - leys in dreams I see,
Cres. f
land of home in dreams I see, And thy hearth fires rise, And,
blue as skies, Eyes of the dear ones are turned on me. Land of home, my
pp Fair flow thy streams, And in sun - lit gleams Break up - on the stones of a
Dolce.
Cres.
land of home, my land of home, my land of home, my
pp Fair flow thy streams, And in sun - lit gleams Break up - on the stones of a
land of home, my land of home, my land of home, my
milk-white strand;
f
land of home; And, as soft haze fills the range of hills, Fond pray'rs arise for my
milk-white strand;
land of home;
f
own loved land. The hills re-sound with song, As we proud-ly march a -

long, For, as of old our sires were bold, Stout hearts have we; While
Cam-bria's moun-tains stand Like the ram-parts of the land, Un-
fet-ter'd as the winds are her chil-dren free! The hills, the
hills re-sound with song, the hills re-sound with
the hills re-
re-sound with
Accel.
song, with song, with song.
sound, the hills re-sound with song.
song, with song, with song.

Chick-a-dee.

James Richardson. Theodore E. Perkins, by per.

1. Twen-ty lit-tle chick-a-dees, Sit-ting in a row; Twen-ty pairs of nak-ed feet, Bur-ied in the snow! I should think you'd fly a-way Where the weather's warm; Then you would not have to be Out there in the storm.
2. Sor-ry lit-tle chick-a-dees! Don't you know the way? Can't you find the road to go Where it's al-ways May? Rob-ins all have found it out, Wrens and blue-birds too: Don't you wish you'd thought to ask, Ere a-way they flew?
3. Hun-gry lit-tle chick-a-dees! Would you like some bread? I will give you all you want, Or some seeds in-stead; A-ny-thing you like to eat, You shall have it free, Ev-ery morning, ev-ery night, If you'll come to me.
4. Jol-ly lit-tle chick-a-dees! Have you had e-nough? Don't for-get to come a-gain While the weather's rough: Bye-bye, hap-py lit-tle birds! Off the wee things swarm, Dancing through the driving snow, Singing in the storm.
Chick-a-dee, chick-a-dee, Pret-ty chick-a-dee,

No, No, No! 167

Grace J. Frances. Hubert P. Main.

1. When by oth-ers urged to tread A path you should not go, Let them blame you,
2. With a frank and hon-est face The wary tempter meet, Nev-er try to
3. When you feel a course is wrong, And conscience tells you so; Tho' a friend should
if they will, But firm-ly an-swer No! Do the right with all your might, A
screen yourself By falsehood's vain de-ceit; Tell the truth whate'er you do, The
bid you err, Be firm and an-swer No! Thus in ev-ery step of life A
pure ex-am-ple show. Nor fear to speak that lit-tle word— No! No!
truth wher-e'er you go; &c.
pure ex-am-ple show: &c.
No! Nor fear to speak that lit-tle word— No! No! No!

Memories of Childhood.

H. R. Palmer.
Meyerbeer, arr. by H. R. Palmer, by per.
Soprano Solo Obligato.
1. I love to roam.......... thro' for - est bow'rs,........ Or sit with -
2. O hap - py time.......... of childish glee,.......... Thou dost a -
1. I love to roam thro' for-est bow'rs,
2. O hap - py time of childish glee,
in........... the qui - et shade,........ And muse up-on........... the by - gone
lone.......... in mem'ry live;.......... Thy brightness oft.......... comes back to
Or sit within the qui - et shade, And muse upon
Thou dost alone in mem'ry live; Thy brightness oft
hours,........ When we as art - - less children played. The sun now
me, ... And yields a joy.......... nought else can give. Our hearts are
the by-gone hours, When we as artless children, artless children played.
comes back to me, And yields a joy nought else can give, nought else can give.

seems........ less bright and fair,........ And flowers shed......... perfume less
bound........ with chains of gold,....... Whose links so bright....... can ne'er grow
The sun now seems less bright and fair And flowers shed
Our hearts are bound with chains of gold— Whose links so bright
rare Than when in childhood.... We roam'd the wildwood,.. With-out a
old, To thy sweet bowers...... O childhood hours!.... Those scenes whose
perfume less rare Childhood hours! Wildwood bow'rs!
can ne'er grow old, Fai - ry bow'rs! Hap - py hours!
thought............. of com-ing care, With-out a thought of com-ing
joy.................. can ne'er be told, Those scenes whose joy can ne'er be
With-out a thought of com-ing care, With-out a thought of com-ing
Those scenes whose joy can ne'er be told, Those scenes whose joy can ne'er be

SOPRANO, ALTO, TENOR & BASE. All sing in unison.
care.... I love to roam...... thro' for-est bow'rs,..... Or sit with-
told.... O hap-py time...... of child-ish glee,....... Thou dost a-
care....
told....
in......... the qui-et shade,...... And muse up-on........ the by-gone
lone....... in mem'ry live;........ Thy brightness oft.......... comes back to
hours,...... When we as art - - less chil-dren played.
me,........ And yields a joy.......... nought else can give.

Home Returning.

THEO. F. SEWARD, by per.

With strong accent.
1. Home re - turn - ing from a - far, Heart with joy up - lift - ed high,
2. Oth - er lands have trea - sure vast, Home a - lone has love to share,
p
Yon - der see the guid-ing star, O what pleasure draweth nigh; Long I've wandered
Now for-get - ting all the past, In the joy that waits me there; Ma - ny years have
sad and lone, Home and dear ones far a - way, From my heart all hope had flown,
passed a - way, Wea - ry years they've been to me, Wait - ing for this hap - py day,
f Cres.
Wel - come now this hap - py day; Home re-turning from a - far, Hearts with joy up-
Home be - lov - ed now I see; Home, &c.
lift - ed high, Yon - der see the guid - ing star, O, what pleasure draweth nigh.

172 All by the Shady Greenwood Tree.

ROSSINI.
Allegretto mosso. f
All by the sha - dy greenwood tree, The mer - ry, mer - ry archers roam;
Jo - vial and bold, and ev - er free, They tread their wood - land home;
p
Rov - ing beneath the moon's soft light, Or in the thick, em - bowering shade,
List'ning the tale, with dear de - light, Of a wand - 'ring syl - van maid:
p
All by the sha - dy greenwood tree, The mer - ry, mer - ry arch - es roam;

f

Jo - vial and bold, and ev - er free, They tread their woodland home!

Jo - vial and bold, and ev - er, ev - er free, They tread, they tread, they

tread their woodland home, they tread their woodland home, their woodland home.

Pastorale.

Gently. GLUCK.

p

1. { O sweet, O sweet, when first the sun Comes laughing out his course to run:
   When night so drear and dawn so gray Blush o'er with joy to yield him way: }
2. { O sweet, O sweet, when first the sun His day-long course has spent and run:
   When cottage roofs with smoke are crown'd, When stars come blinking out a-round: }
3. { O sweet, O sweet, who's life's first morn The smiles of blameless mirth a - dorn:
   Whose widening years with joy are fraught From wisdom's own clear sunshine caught: }

When larks mount high and lin - nets sing, And all things give their wel - com-ing.
When birds with song re - seek their nest, And all things fold themselves to rest.
Who sleep be - neath the pure de - fence, Life wins in Age from in - no - cence.

174 Where is my Boy To-night?

With Tenderness.
Words and Music by Rev. Robert Lowry, by per.
1. Where is my wand'ring boy to-night—The boy of my tend'rest care, The boy that was once my joy and light, The child of my love and prayer?
2. Once he was pure as morn-ing dew, As he knelt at his moth-er's knee; No face was so bright, no heart more true, And none was so sweet as he.
3. O could I see you now, my boy, As fair as in old - en time, When prat - tle and smile made home a joy, And life was a mer - ry chime!
4. Go for my wand'ring boy to-night; Go, search for him where you will; But bring him to me with all his blight, And tell him I love him still.
Chorus. Not too fast.
O where is my boy to - night? O where is my boy to - night? My

Published in Sheet form by Biglow & Main.

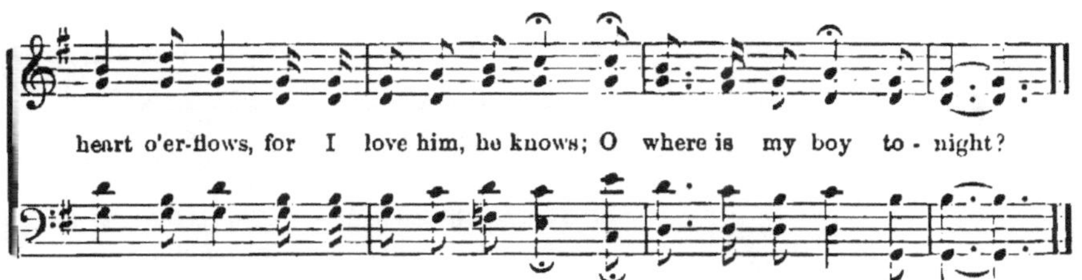
heart o'er-flows, for I love him, he knows; O where is my boy to - night?

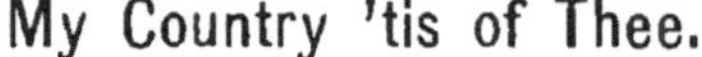
My Country 'tis of Thee.

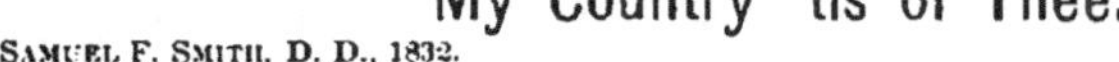
SAMUEL F. SMITH, D. D., 1832. Dr. JOHN BULL.

1. My country 'tis of thee, Sweet land of lib - er - ty, Of thee I sing; Land where my
2. My na - tive country, thee, Land of the no - ble, free, Thy name I love; I love thy
3. Let mu-sic swell the breeze, And ring from all the trees Sweet freedom's song: Let mor - tal
4. Our fa-ther's God, to Thee, Au - thor of lib - er - ty, To Thee we sing: Long may our

fathers died, Land of the pilgrims' pride, From every mountain side Let freedom ring.
rocks and rills, Thy woods and templed hills; My heart with rapture thrills Like that a - bove.
tongues awake, Let all that breathe partake, Let rocks their silence break, The sound prolong.
land be bright With freedom's holy light; Protect us by Thy might, Great God, our King!

Sweet is the Hour. (Round.)

Sweet is the hour of twi - light grey, When eve - ning veils the face of day;

When shades of night be - gin to fall, The dark-ness soon will cov - er all.

Sabbath Morn.

MENDELSSOHN.

Andante Sostenuto,
Cres.
1. This is the Sabbath morn, This is the Sabbath
2. Kneeling I pray to thee! Kneeling I pray to
p
f
p
Cres.
f
morn; I am a - lone.... with-in the dell, Yet one faint sound, the mat - in
thee! Soft breezes breathe a hallowed sound, I feel as though all na - ture
pp
Cres.
Dim.
bell; Now still.... is wood and lawn, Now still is wood and lawn.
round Were bound in pray'r with me, Were bound in pray'r with me.

Cres.
p
3. A-bove what glo-ries play, A - bove what glories play, Seeming as
Cres.
p
pp
though the fields of light Were o - pen to my wondering sight, This
Cres.
pp
sf
.... is the Sabbath day! This...... is the Sabbath day!
Cres.
f
p

178

I Would that my Love.

HEINRICH HEINE.
DUET.
MENDELSSOHN.
Allegretto con moto.
1. I would that my love could si - lent - ly
2. To thee on their wings, my fair - est that
flow.... in a sin - gle word,
soul - felt word they would bear,
I'd give it the mer - ry
Should'st hear it at ev - 'ry
bree - z - es, They'd waft it a - way in sport,
mo - ment, And hear...... it ev - 'ry where,
Cres - cen - do.
I'd
Should'st
give it the mer - ry breez - es, They'd waft it a-way in
hear it at ev - 'ry mo - ment, And hear..... it ev - 'ry

sport, a - way in sport,... a - way in sport,... They'd
where, and ev - 'ry where, .. and ev - 'ry where, .. And
waft it a - way in sport.
hear..... it ev - 'ry where.
sf
sf
pp
3. At night..... when thine eye-lids in slum - ber have
pp
clos'd those bright heav'nly beams, Still there, my love, it will
sempre. pp
Cres

Cres - - - - cen - - - do.
haunt thee...... e'en in thy deep-est dreams,.. Still
- - - - cen - - - - - - - - - - do.
f
there, my love,... it will haunt thee, e'en in...... thy deep-est
f
p
dreams, E'en in thy deep - est, thy deep-est dreams, E'en
in...... thy deepest, deep - - est dreams.
pp

Sound the Battle Cry!

Wm. F. Sherwin.
Wm. F. Sherwin, by per.
Vigorously, in march time.
1. Sound the bat - tle cry! See the foe is nigh; Raise the standard high
2. Strong to meet the foe, Marching on we go, While our cause we know
3. Oh! Thou God of all, Hear us when we call; Help us one and all
For the Lord; Gird your ar - mor on, Stand firm ev - ery one; Rest your
Must pre - vail; Shield and ban - ner bright Gleaming in the light; Bat - tling
By Thy grace; When the bat - tle's done, And the vict - 'ry won, May we
cause up-on His ho - ly word.
for the right We ne'er can fail.
wear the crown Be-fore Thy throne.
Chorus. ff
Rouse then, soldiers! ral - ly round the ban - ner!
Read - y, stead - y, pass the word a - long; On - ward, for - ward,
shout a - loud Ho - san - na! Christ is Cap - tain of the might - y throng.

Jennie Lee.

F. J. C. THEODORE E. PERKINS.

1. Winning every bird and blossom, In her sport - ive glee, Pride of all the
2. I have seen her gai - ly roaming With the sum-mer bee, I have heard her
3. By the myrtle, in the valley, There she waits for me, When the bon-nie
vil - lage maidens, Darling Jen - nie Lee; Blushing like the modest ros - es,
'witching mu - sic, Darling Jen - nie Lee; Tripping where the i - dle zeph - yr
moon is shining, Darling Jen - nie Lee; She, the flower I long have cher - ished,
Ad lib.
Smil-ing with de-light, Dimpled cheek and lips of cor - al, Brow of snowy white.
Drinks the morning dew, Tell - ing tales of mirth and gladness, In her eye of blue.
Blooming all for me, Sim - ple hearted, trusting maiden, Darling Jen-nie Lee.
Chorus.
Pret - ty Jen - nie, play - ful Jen-nie, O so dear to me,

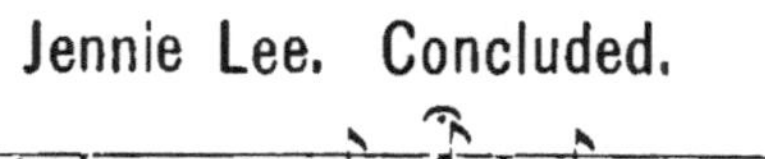

Fair - est of the vil - lage maidens, Dar - ling Jen - nie Lee.

Return to School.

F. J. C.

Old College Song.

ff ALL.

Girls. 1. To school and its pleasures a - gain we re - turn, Sing with a mer-ry cheer!
Boys. 2. How pleasant the summer, and full of de - light, Sing with a mer-ry cheer!

ff ALL.

A - gain we as - sem - ble our les - sons to learn, Sing with a mer - ry cheer!
The au - tumn is com-ing so tran-quil and bright, Sing with a mer - ry cheer!

First time f, second p.

Hap - py va - ca - tion, how quick-ly it passed! Hol - i - day rambles are
Faith-ful in - structors, a greeting for you! Let us in earn - est our

o - ver at last; Welcome to all! Welcome to all! Sing with a merry cheer!
la - bors pur - sue; Welcome to all! Welcome to all! Sing with a merry cheer!

The Village of the Vale.

THEODORE E. PERKINS, by per.
1. Lit-tle vale with fair-y mea-dows, Trees that spread your leaf-y hands,
2. In thy green and sun-ny pas-tures, Near thy bright and gras-sy streams,
FINE.
Flow-ers clothed in soft-est beau-ty, Love-li-er than east-ern lands.
Free from care we love to wan-der, Cheered by sum-mer's ra-diant beams.
Vil-lage home of ev-ery treas-ure, Thee we sing in strains of pleas-ure,
Scenes of sweet-est re-col-lec-tion, Sa-cred to the soul's re-flec-tion,
D. C. 1st Verse.
Vil-lage in the si-lent vale, Love-ly vil-lage, thee we hail.
Try, Try Again.
CHARLES W. SANDERS.
WM. B. BRADBURY, by per.
1. 'Tis a les-son you should heed, Try, try a-gain; If at first you
2. Once or twice tho' you should fail, Try, try a-gain; If at last you
3. If you find your task is hard, Try, try a-gain; Time will bring you

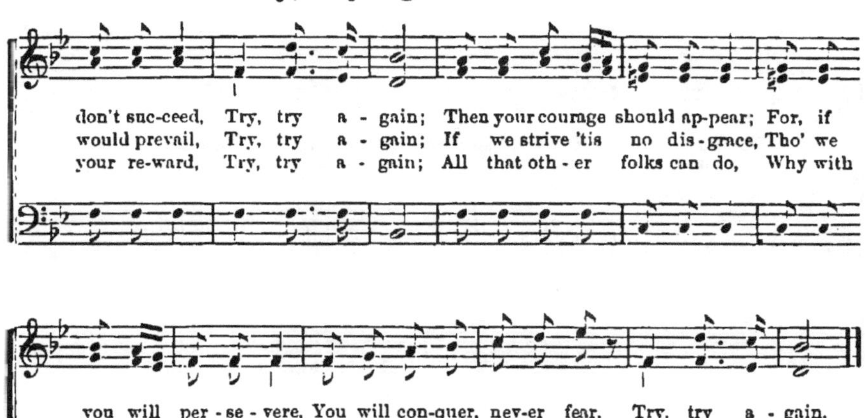
don't suc-ceed, Try, try a - gain; Then your courage should ap-pear; For, if
would prevail, Try, try a - gain; If we strive 'tis no dis-grace, Tho' we
your re-ward, Try, try a - gain; All that oth - er folks can do, Why with

you will per - se - vere, You will con-quer, nev-er fear. Try, try a - gain.
may not win the race; What should you do in that case? Try, try a - gain.
pa - tience may not you? On - ly keep this rule in view, Try, try a - gain.

The Coming Spring.

Wm. B. Bradbury, by per.

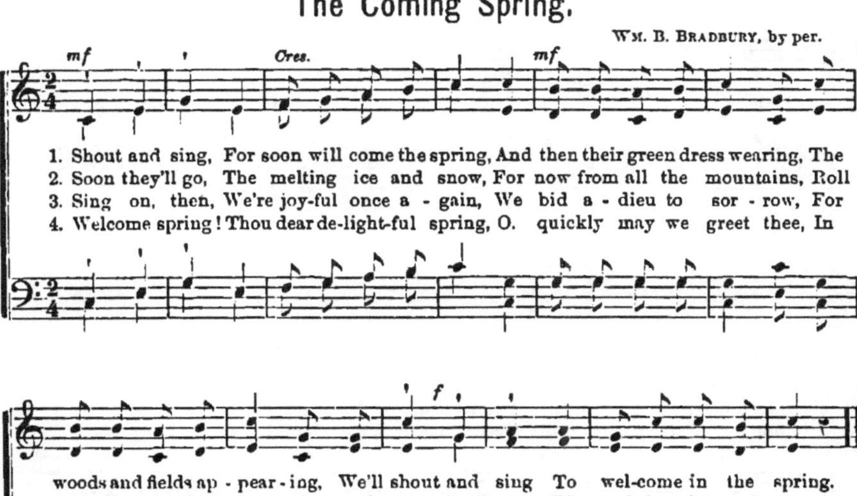
mf
Cres.
mf
1. Shout and sing, For soon will come the spring, And then their green dress wearing, The
2. Soon they'll go, The melting ice and snow, For now from all the mountains, Roll
3. Sing on, then, We're joy-ful once a - gain, We bid a - dieu to sor - row, For
4. Welcome spring! Thou dear de-light-ful spring, O. quickly may we greet thee, In
f
woods and fields ap - pear - ing, We'll shout and sing To wel-come in the spring.
down the smaller foun-tains, And soon they'll go, The melt-ing ice and snow.
hope gilds ev - ery mor-row, Sing on, sing on, We're joy-ful once a - gain.
field and gar-den meet thee, Then wel-come, spring, Thou dear, de-light-ful spring!

Oh, I'd be a Fairy.

FANNY J. CROSBY.
HUBERT P. MAIN, by per.
SOLO—TREBLE.
1. Oh, I'd be a fair - y, so grace-ful and air - y, And dance with the
2. Oh, I'd be a fair - y, so grace-ful and air - y, I'd come when the
ALTO—Voice accomp.
La la la la la la la la la la la la la la la
TENOR.
BASE.
brooklet that ripples for me; I'd play with a zeph-yr, and when I was
D.S. I'd trip o'er the lawn when the day-light was
days of the summer were long; I'd steal o'er the meadows where daisies were
D.S. Then soft-ly I'd whisper, and touch with my
la la la la la la la. La la la la la la la la la la
FINE.
wea - ry, The bell of a lil - y my cra - dle should be. I'd float on a
fad - ing, And jew - el my hair with a pearl from the dew.
blooming, And roam in the greenwood with beauty and song. Un - seen I would
fing - er The springs of the heart that by sorrow were bound.
la la la la la la la la la la la la la. Oh, I'd be a

D. C.
beam from the eye of the morning, And spangle my wing with its bright rosy hue;
vis - it the home of the lone-ly, And scatter the garlands of pleasure around,
fair - y, Yes, I'd be a fair - y, Yes, I'd be a fair - y, a fair - y I'd be.
Little Bo-Peep.
J. W. Elliott.
p Andante quasi Allegretto.
1. Lit - tle Bo - Peep has lost her sheep, And can't tell where to find them;
2. Lit - tle Bo - Peep fell fast a - sleep, And dreamt she heard them bleat-ing;
3 Then up she took her lit - tle crook, De - ter - mined sure to find them;
p
Cres.
f
Dim.
Leave them a - lone, and they'll come home, Wagging their tails be - hind them.
When she a - woke 'twas all a joke, Ah! cru - el vision so fleet - ing.
What was her joy to be - hold them nigh, Wagging their tails be - hind them.
Cres.
fz
Dim.

188
Nancy Lee.
Fred. E. Weatherly, M. A.
Stephen Adams.
With Spirit.
1. Of all the wives as e'er you know, ... Yeo ho! lads! ho! Yeo ho! yeo ho! There's none like Nancy Lee I trow, ... Yeo ho! lads! ho! yeo ho! See, there she stands an' waves her hands, upon the
2. The har - bor's past, the breezes blow, ... Yeo ho! lads! ho! Yeo ho! yeo ho! 'Tis long ere we come back, I know; ...... Yeo ho! lads! ho! yeo ho! But true an' bright from morn till night my home will
3. The boa' - s'n pipes the watch be - low, ... Yeo ho! lads! ho! Yeo ho! yeo ho! Then here's a health a-fore we go, ... Yeo ho! lads! ho! yeo ho! A long, long life to my sweet wife, an' mates at

quay, An' ev'-ry day when I'm a-way, She'll watch for me, An'
be, An' all so neat, an' snug an' sweet for Jack, at sea, An'
sea; An' keep our bones from Davy Jones wher-e'er we be, An'
whisper low, when tempests blow, for Jack, at sea, Yeo ho! lads! ho! yeo
Nan-cy's face to bless the place, an' wel - come me; Yeo ho! lads! ho! yeo
may you meet a mate as sweet as Nan - cy Lee; Yeo ho! lads! ho! yeo
Refrain.* Solo, Voice Accompaniment.
ho! The sail - or's wife the sail-or's star shall be, Yeo ho! we
The sailor's wife the sailor's star, his star shall be, Yeo ho! Yeo ho! we
go a - cross the sea,..... The sail - or's wife the sail - or's
go, yeo ho! a-cross the sea, the sea, The sail-or's wife his star shall

* Arr. of Chorus, Copyright, 1880, by Biglow & Main.

Nancy Lee. Concluded.
star...... shall be, The sail - or's wife his star shall be.........
be, his star shall be, The sail - or's wife his star shall be.........
Farewell to Winter.
Wm. B. Bradbury, by per.
f Joyfully.
Repeat ff
O-pen wide the doors, sing a-loud for joy, Be lively, boys, be lively, boys, be lively;
1. Old crabbed Win-ter must de-part, He packs his rub-bish, loth to start, And
2. He scents the spring on ev - ery gale, And turns, with ter-ror, weak and pale; The
3. For Spring is here, al - rea-dy here—I hear her voice, so sweet and clear; And
4. The spring-birds raise a joy-ful strain, I hear the rea - dy, sweet re - frain, An
loi - ters round from room to room, With coughs, and sighs, and looks of gloom. Be
poor old man is filled with fear, He knows his mor - tal foe is near. Be
gen-tly tap-ping, see her stand, With clus-tered flower-buds in her hand. Be
ech - o from each answering breast, Come in, come in, thou wel - come guest. Be

Soon to our Homes we shall Journey.

G. J. F. PARTING SONG. HUBERT P. MAIN.

1. Soon to our homes we shall jour - ney, Dear ones a - gain we shall see;
2. We have been hap - py to - geth - er, Friends and companions so long;
3. Soon to our homes we shall jour - ney, Let us be faith-ful and kind;

Yet we are leav - ing be - hind us Mem'ries that sa - cred will be:
Pure are the links that u - nite us, Links that are hal - lowed and strong:
Then, in the du - ties that wait us, Com-fort and joy we shall find:

Soon to our homes we shall jour - ney, Far from each oth - er to dwell.
How can we break them a - sun - der. Far from each oth - er to dwell,
Think of a re - gion be - yond us,— Live, that our spir - its may dwell,

Sad are the words we are breath-ing, Schoolmates, we bid you fare - well,
Sad are these moments of part - ing, Schoolmates, we bid you fare - well,
Blest by a lov - ing Re - deem-er, Chilled by no part - ing fare - well,

Sad are the words we are breath-ing, Schoolmates, we bid you fare - well.
Sad are these moments of part - ing, Schoolmates, we bid you fare - well.
Blest by a lov - ing Re - deem - er, Chilled by no part - ing fare - well.

Faithful and True.

Richard Wagner.

p
Faith - ful and true now rest you here, Where love triumph - ant shall
Faith - ful and true now rest you here, Where love shall crown..........

crown ye with joy! Star of re - nown, flower of the earth,
.... ye with joy! Star of re - nown, flower of the earth,

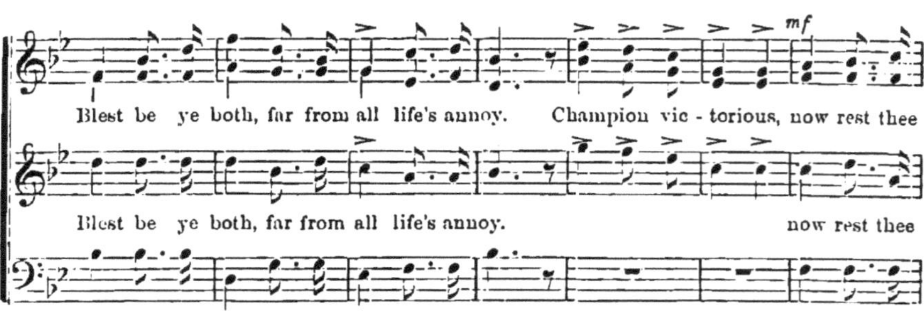
mf
Blest be ye both, far from all life's annoy. Champion vic - torious, now rest thee
Blest be ye both, far from all life's annoy. now rest thee

p
p
here! Maid bright and glorious, now rest thee here! Mirth's noi - sy rev - el
here! now rest thee here! The rev - - - el

ye have for - sak - en,
ye've for - sak - en, Ten-der de-lights for you now a - wak - en! Fragrant a -
ye've for - sak - en, Ten-der de-lights for you now a - wak - en! Fragrant a -
Dim.
p
bode, en-shrine ye in bliss, Splendor of state, in joy ye dis - miss;
bode, en-shrine ye in bliss, Splendor of state, in joy ye dis-miss;
p
Faith-ful and true now rest ye here, Where love triumph - ant shall
Faith-ful and true now rest ye here, Where love shall crown..........
crown ye with joy! Star of re - nown, flower of the earth, Blest be ye
.... ye with joy! Star of re - nown, flower of the earth, Blest be ye

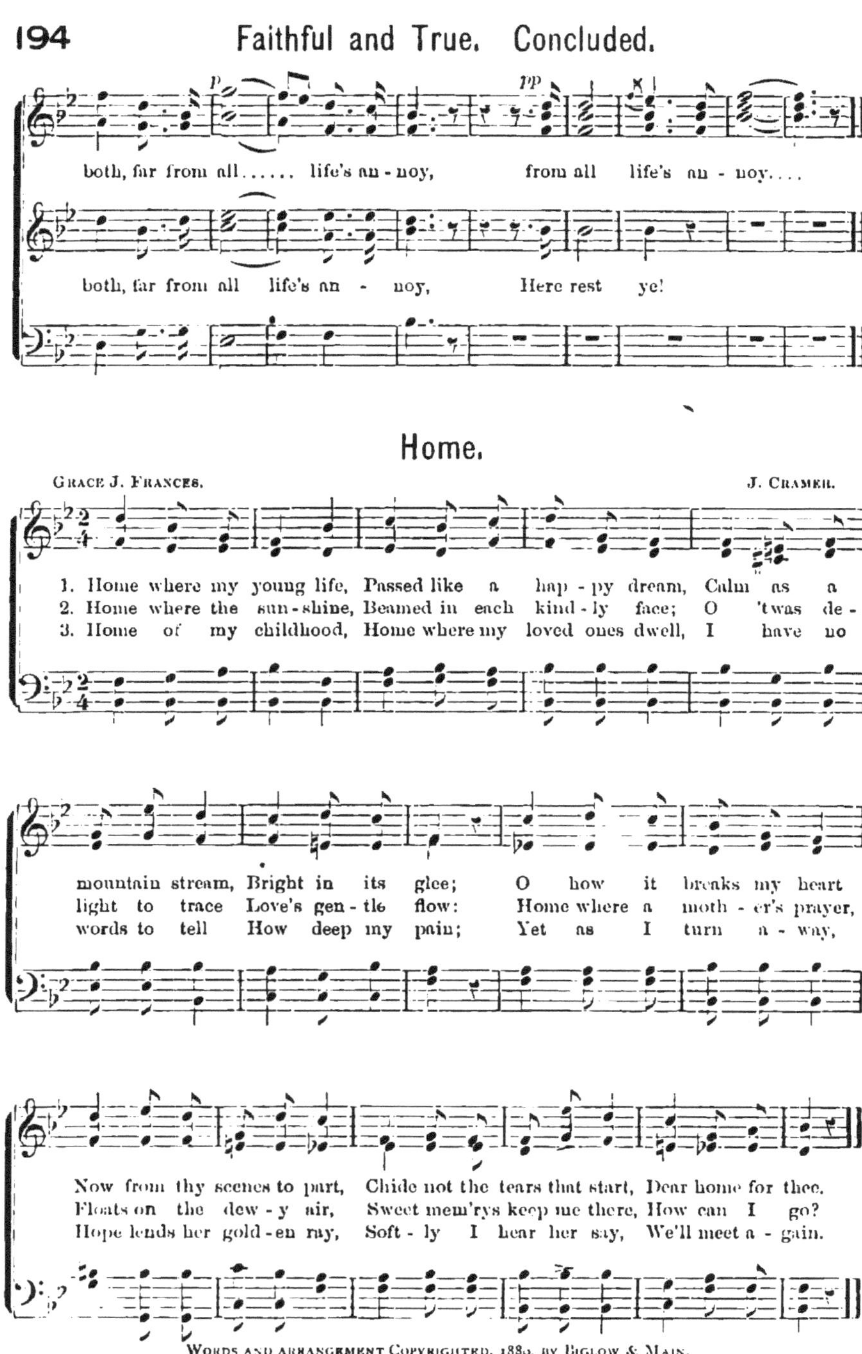
both, far from all...... life's an - noy, from all life's an - noy....
both, far from all life's an - noy, Here rest ye!
Home.
GRACE J. FRANCES.
J. CRAMER.
1. Home where my young life, Passed like a hap - py dream, Calm as a mountain stream, Bright in its glee; O how it breaks my heart Now from thy scenes to part, Chide not the tears that start, Dear home for thee.
2. Home where the sun - shine, Beamed in each kind - ly face; O 'twas de - light to trace Love's gen - tle flow: Home where a moth - er's prayer, Floats on the dew - y air, Sweet mem'rys keep me there, How can I go?
3. Home of my childhood, Home where my loved ones dwell, I have no words to tell How deep my pain; Yet as I turn a - way, Hope lends her gold - en ray, Soft - ly I hear her say, We'll meet a - gain.

Fairy Greeting. 195

FANNY J. CROSBY.
TRIO.
THEODORE E. PERKINS, by per.
1st & 2d SOPRANO.
1. Ye come, and we bid you wel - come; Ye come o'er the o - cean blue,
2. Our wings in a beam of sun - light, That float-ed in i - dle play,
CONTRALTO.
Then haste to our home so love - ly, The bower we have twined for you.
We spangled to make them bril - liant With beau - ty and joy to - day.
For we are the wild-wood fair - ies, In our voice is a dream - y spell,
Then dance with the wildwood fair - ies To the song of the bird and breeze,
And we know where the elves are hiding, In the depths of the mos - sy dell;
As they war - ble so sweet-ly o'er us From the boughs of the for - est trees;
And we know where the elves are hid - ing, In the depths of the mos-sy dell.
As they war-ble so sweet-ly o'er us, From the boughs of the for-est trees.

196

Our Songs of Joy and Gladness.

GREETING SONG. MEYERBEER.

Con Spirito.
pp
1. Our songs of joy, our songs of joy and gladness, We'll sing, we'll sing, we'll sing in cheerful lay, No note of pain, no note of pain or sadness Shall greet, shall greet, shall greet this joyous
2. A-wake! a-wake! a-wake sweet notes of pleasure, In song, in song, in full and joy-ous song, Move on, move on, move on in grace-ful measure, To speed, to speed, to speed the hours a-

day, Yes, then hail this joyous day, Our songs of
long, Speed the hours, the hours a-long, A-wake, a -
Yes, then hail this joy-ous day,
Speed the hours, the hours a - long,
8va
joy, our songs of joy and glad-ness, We'll sing, we'll sing, we'll sing in cheer-ful
wake, a-wake sweet notes of pleasure, In song, in song, in full and joy-ous
8va
lay; No note of pain, no note of pain or sad - ness Shall greet, shall
song; Move on, move on, move on in graceful meas - ure, To speed, to
8va

greet, shall greet this joyous day. This joy - ous day, All hail this joy - ous
speed, to speed the hours a - long.
8va loco.
f
f
day, All hail, all hail, all hail this joy-ous day, all hail this day,
all hail this
all hail this day, this merry, merry, merry, merry, merry, merry, merry,
this happy, happy, happy, happy, happy, happy, happy,
ff
day, all hail this day,
ff

pp
day, Our songs, our songs, our songs of joy and glad-ness, We'll sing, we'll
day. A-wake, a-wake, a-wake sweet notes of pleasure, In full, in
pp
sing, we'll sing in cheerful lay; No note of pain, no note of pain or
full, in full and joy-ous song, Move on, move on, move on in graceful
sad - ness, Shall greet, shall greet, shall greet this happy day.
measure, To speed, to speed, to speed the hours a - long.

Farewell to the Forest.

FELIX MENDELSSOHN BARTHOLDY.

P Andante non Lento.
1. Oh! for-est, deep and gloomy, Oh! woodland, vale, and hill, Of all my joys and
2. The for-est soft - ly whispers In tones of truth-ful might, It speaks of earn-est
3. The tranquil glades now leaving, To dis - tant lands I roam, Life's anxious toil pur-
When sick of worldly pleas - ures,
sorrows The gen - tle wit - ness still; When sick of world - - ly pleas - ures,
du - ty, Of what is wrong and right; I lis - ten to its teach - ing
su - ing 'Mid strangers seek a home; Tho' far from hence.... re - pin - ing,
Tho' far from hence repining,
Leav-ing the bu - sy town, I seek thy qui - et shad - ows, And, wea-ry, lay me
With patient, humble ear, To me the beauteous language Shall be for ev - er
Thrown 'mong the worldlings cold, Fond mem'ry still shall charm me, My heart shall ne'er grow
shad - - - ows, I
lan - - - guage, To
charm me, Fond
down I seek thy qui - et shad - ows. And, weary, lay me down.
dear; To me the beauteous lan - guage Shall be for - ev - - - - er dear.
old, Fond mem'ry still shall charm me, My heart..... shall ne'er grow old.
seek thy qui - et shad - - ows, And, weary, lay me down.
me thy beauteous lan - - guage, Shall be for - ev - - - - er dear.
mem'ry still shall charm me, My heart shall ne'er grow old.

The Distant Chimes.

TRIO FOR FEMALE VOICES.

J. E. CARPENTER. STEPHEN GLOVER.

The dis - tant chimes.. at e - ven tide, When list - 'ning to their
p
a tempo.
sound,........ As o'er the stream.... it seems to glide, What
mf
con espress.
va - ried thoughts a-bound! What va - ried thoughts a - bound!... They give to
They give to
mf

1st SOP.
Hope...... her wonted sway, They gild the past...... with mem'ry's ray,.... All, all we
2d SOP.
Hope...... her wonted sway, They gild the past...... with mem'ry's ray,.... All, all we
ALTO.
They give to Hope her wonted sway, They gild the past with mem'ry's ray,
p
Ped. Ped. Ped. Ped.

lov'd...... in olden times, They now recall, sweet dis - tant chimes.
lov'd...... in olden times, They now recall, sweet dis - tant chimes.
All, all we lov'd in olden times, re-call, sweet dis - tant chimes.
Ped. Ped. Ped. Ped. Cres.

2d SOP.
Piu animato.
Oh! life is like that sunny stream O'er which the day-light
ALTO.
Piu animato.
sf dim. p
Ped.
fades;.... And those sweet chimes are like the dream.... That all our past per-
Ped.
1st SOP.
The shades of night will close a-round, The tuneful chimes soon cease to sound, And all on
2d SOP.
vades: The shades of night will close a-round, The tuneful chimes soon cease to sound, And all on
ALTO.

Dim. Rit. a tempo.
which fond mem'ry dwells, Be si - lent as those distant bells,
which fond mem'ry dwells, Be si - lent as those distant bells,
which fond mem'ry dwells, Be si - lent as those distant bells, Be silent as those distant
p
Dim. Rit. a tempo. tranquillo.
p
Dim.
Hark! Hark! Hark still down the
p
Hark! Hark! Hark still down the
Dim.
bells, Be silent as those distant bells,
Dim. Rit. pp

Con espress.
stream........ they seem to glide, Sweet distant chimes........ at e - ven
stream........ they seem to glide, Sweet distant chimes........ at e - ven
still down the stream they seem to glide, Sweet distant chimes,
Ped. * Ped. * Ped. *
tide,......... Still down the stream........ they seem to glide, Sweet distant
tide,......... Still down the stream........ they seem to glide, Sweet distant
at e - ven tide, Still down the stream they seem to glide, Sweet
Ped. * Ped. * Ped. *

Dol.
Cres.
chimes at e - ven tide, . . Hark! hark! those chimes . . make tuneful rhymes . . Those distant
chimes at e - ven tide, ... Hark! hark! Hark! hark! those distant
chimes at e - ven tide, ... Hark! hark! those chimes make tuneful rhymes, those distant
Ped. ✲ Ped. ✲ Ped. ✲ Ped. Cres. ✲
Cres.
chimes make tuneful rhymes, Hark! hark! those chimes make tuneful rhymes, Those distant
chimes make tune-ful rhymes, Hark! hark! Hark! hark! those distant
chimes make tune-ful rhymes, Hark! hark! those chimes make tuneful rhymes, those distant
Ped. Decres. ✲ Ped. ✲ Ped. ✲ Ped. ✲ Ped. ✲

poco a poco dim.
chimes make tune - ful rhymes,...... Sweet distant chimes,...... Sweet distant
chimes make tune - ful rhymes,...... Sweet distant chimes,...... Sweet distant
chimes make tune - ful rhymes........ Sweet distant chimes,
poco a poco dim.
Ped.
Decres.
p lento.
chimes,..........Sweet distant chimes..........................
chimes,..........Sweet distant chimes..........................
Sweet distant chimes, Sweet dis - tant chimes.
lento.
pp
Rit.
Ped.

208 Parting Song.

Prof. Homer B. Sprague.
Hubert P. Main, by per.
Con espressione.
1. Not a link of love is bro - ken, Nor its chain less bright and strong,
2. Lo! the pres - ent! cheering voi - ces Bid us la - bor morn and noon;
3. Break the chain of hate and ter - ror, Lift the fall - en, ban - ish pain;
4. We are part - ing, we are part - ing, Hushed the voice, the vis - ion o'er;
Tho' the last good - bye is spo - ken, And we breathe our fare - well song;
Bid us hush the jar - ring nois - es Mingling with earth's sweetest tune;
Light the dark, tread down the er - ror, Win by love, live not in vain;
Sighs are heav - ing, tears are start - ing, We may meet on earth no more;
On the Past, how Mem'ry lin - gers, Tell - ing oft of du - ties done!
Hark! Hu - man - i - ty is call - ing— "Live, work, battle for the Right;
Faint not, rest not, work thy mis - sion, Ev - er pur - er, stron - ger rise,
But somewhere in yon blue heav - en, Far a - bove earth's din and storm,
Lo! the Fu - ture! Hope's bright fingers Lift new crowns, and beck - on on.
Stand for Truth, its friends are fall - ing, Take their pla - ces in the fight."
Till at last the gates E - ly - sian, Flash in splen - dor thro' the skies.
Friends who now from friends are riv - en, See for aye each van - ished form.

Gloria Patri.

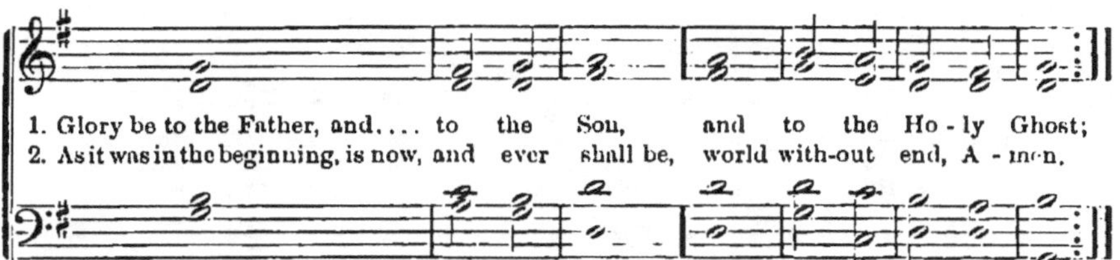
1. Glory be to the Father, and.... to the Son, and to the Ho - ly Ghost;
2. As it was in the beginning, is now, and ever shall be, world with-out end, A - men.

God of my Life.

Glaser.

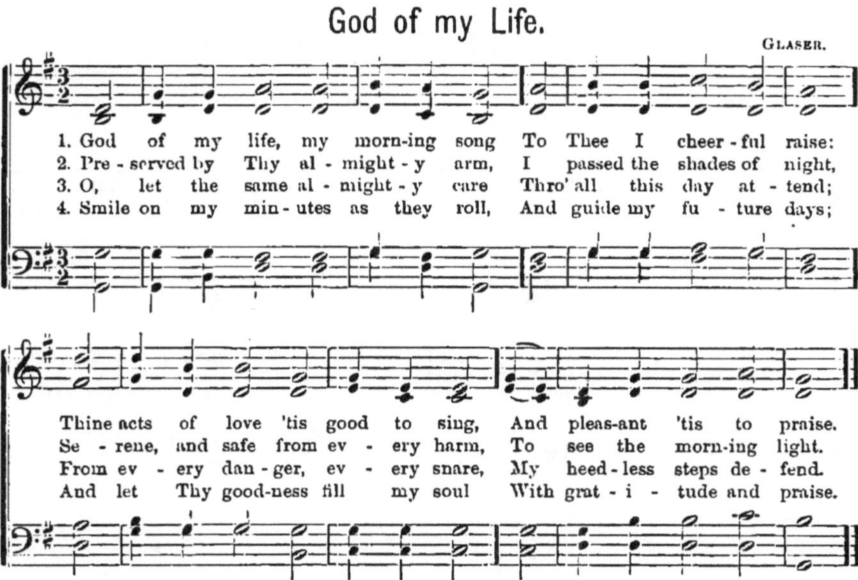
1. God of my life, my morn-ing song To Thee I cheer - ful raise:
2. Pre - served by Thy al - might - y arm, I passed the shades of night,
3. O, let the same al - might - y care Thro' all this day at - tend;
4. Smile on my min - utes as they roll, And guide my fu - ture days;
Thine acts of love 'tis good to sing, And pleas-ant 'tis to praise.
Se - rene, and safe from ev - ery harm, To see the morn-ing light.
From ev - ery dan - ger, ev - ery snare, My heed - less steps de - fend.
And let Thy good-ness fill my soul With grat - i - tude and praise.

The Lord's Prayer.

Gregorian.

1. Our Father, who art in heaven, | hallowed | be Thy | name; || Thy kingdom come, Thy will be done on | earth...as it | is in | heaven;
2. Give us this | day our | daily | bread; || And forgive us our debts, as | we for- | give our | debtors.
3. And lead us not into temptation, but de- | liver | us from | evil: || For Thine is the kingdom, and the power, and the glory, for- | ever. | A- | men.

Universal Chorus.

Edwin F. Hatfield, D. D., 1837. Wm. B. Bradbury, by per.

Allegro.

1. Hal - le - lu - jah!—praise the Lord; Sing Mes - si - ah's glo - ry;
Heaven and earth! with one ac - cord, Shout the wondrous sto - ry;
Praise Him for His might - y deeds, Praise ye Him, whose grace ex - ceeds
All that heaven in song con - cedes; Worlds of bliss! His praise re - cord.

2. Praise Him with the trumpet's tongue, Far and wide re - sound - ing;
Praise Him with the harp well strung, While your hearts are bounding;
Praise Him with the sweet-toned lyre; Let His praise the lute in - spire;
Praise Him in a might - y choir;—Let His praise be loud - ly sung.

3. Praise Him with the vi - ol's strings, Wak - ing joy - ous feel - ing
While the vault of glo - ry rings With the or - gan's peal - ing;
Let the cym - bals ring His praise, Wake the clar - ion's grand-est lays,
Praise the Lord thro' end - less days;—Him the wide cre - a - tion sings.

Old Hundred. L. M.

Praise God from whom all blessings flow, Praise Him, all creatures here be - low;
Praise Him a - bove, ye heavenly host; Praise Fa - ther, Son, and Ho - ly Ghost.

My Saviour Dear.

F. T. PALGRAVE. THEODORE E. PERKINS, by per.

1. Thou that once on moth-er's knee Wert a lit - tle one like me,
2. Be be - side me in the light, Close be - side me all the night,
When I wake or go to bed, Lay Thy hand a - bout my head; Let me feel Thee
Make me gen - tle, kind and true, Do what mother bids me do. Help and cheer me
ve - ry near, Je - sus Christ, my Sav-iour dear.
when I fret, And for-give when I for - get.
1. Day by day the man - na fell; Oh, to learn this les - son well!
2. "Day by day," the prom-ise reads, Dai - ly strength for dai - ly needs;
3. Thou our dai - ly task shalt give; Day by day to Thee we live;
Still by con - stant mer - cy fed, Give us, Lord, our dai - ly bread.
Cast fore-bod - ing fear a - way, Take the man - na of to - day.
So shall add - ed years ful - fil Not our own, our Fa - ther's will.

3 Thou art near me when I pray,
Though Thou art so far away;
Thou my little hymn wilt hear,
Jesus Christ, my Saviour dear.
Thou that once on mother's knee
Wert a little one like me.

Day by Day the Manna Fell.

REV. JOSIAH CONDER. LOUIS MOREAU GOTTSCHALK, 1856.

In Heavenly Love Abiding.

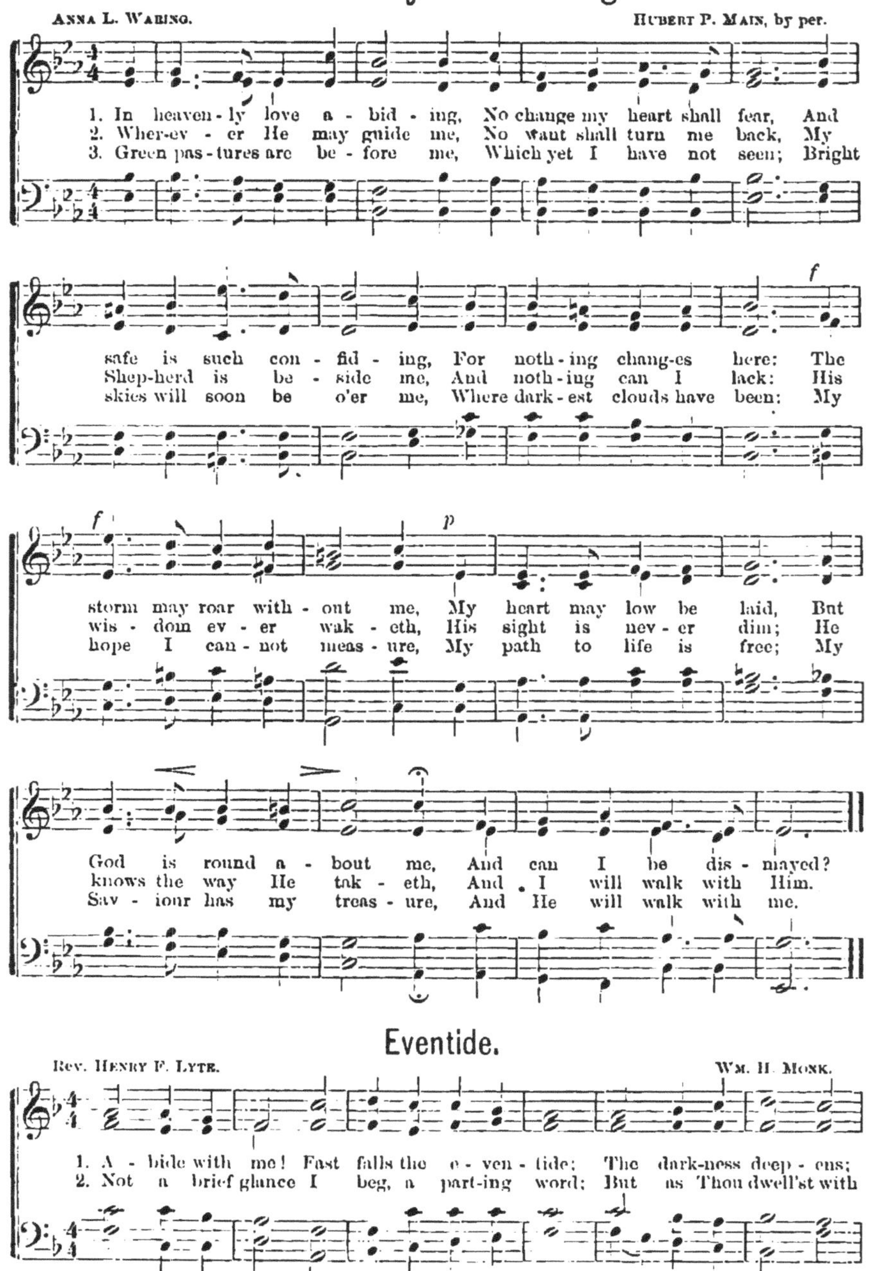
ANNA L. WARING.
HUBERT P. MAIN, by per.
1. In heaven-ly love a - bid - ing, No change my heart shall fear, And
2. Wher-ev - er He may guide me, No want shall turn me back, My
3. Green pas-tures are be - fore me, Which yet I have not seen; Bright
safe is such con - fid - ing, For noth-ing chang-es here: The
Shep-herd is be - side me, And noth-ing can I lack: His
skies will soon be o'er me, Where dark-est clouds have been: My
f
storm may roar with - out me, My heart may low be laid, But
wis - dom ev - er wak - eth, His sight is nev - er dim; He
hope I can - not meas - ure, My path to life is free; My
p
God is round a - bout me, And can I be dis - mayed?
knows the way He tak - eth, And I will walk with Him.
Sav - iour has my treas - ure, And He will walk with me.
Eventide.
REV. HENRY F. LYTE.
WM. H. MONK.
1. A - bide with me! Fast falls the e - ven - tide; The dark-ness deep - ens;
2. Not a brief glance I beg, a part-ing word; But as Thou dwell'st with

Lord, with me a - bide! When oth - er help - ers fail, and com-forts flee,
Thy dis - ci - ples, Lord, Fa - mil-iar, con - de - scend-ing, pa - tient, free;
Help of the help - less, O a - bide with me!
Come, not to so - journ, but a - bide with me! A - men.
O Holy Saviour!
Charlotte Elliott, 1834.
F. F. Flemming.
1. O ho - ly Sav - iour! Friend un - seen, Since on Thine arm Thou
2. What tho' the world de - ceit - ful prove, And earthly friends and
bidst me lean; Help me throughout life's chang-ing scene,
hopes re - move; With pa - tient, un - com - plain - ing love
By faith to cling to Thee.
Still would I cling to Thee.
3 If e'er I seem to tread alone
Life's weary waste, with thorns o'ergrown;
Thy voice of love in gentlest tone,
Still whispers, "cling to Me!"
4 If faith and hope are often tried,
I'll ask not, need not aught beside;
So safe, so calm, so satisfied,
The soul that clings to Thee!

Closing Hymn.

Rev. John Ellerton. Edward J. Hopkins.

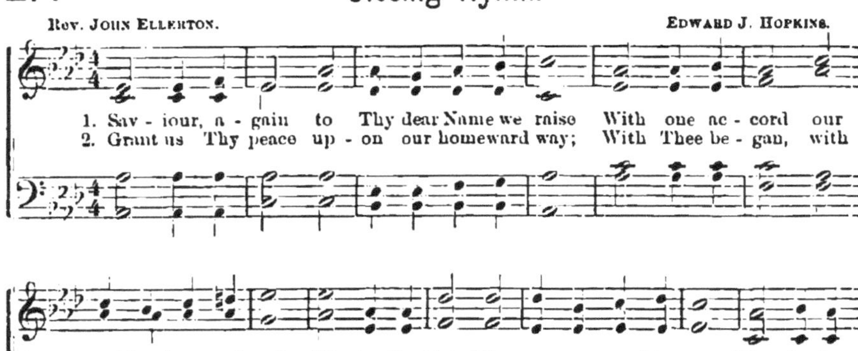
1. Sav - iour, a - gain to Thy dear Name we raise With one ac - cord our
2. Grant us Thy peace up - on our homeward way; With Thee be - gan, with

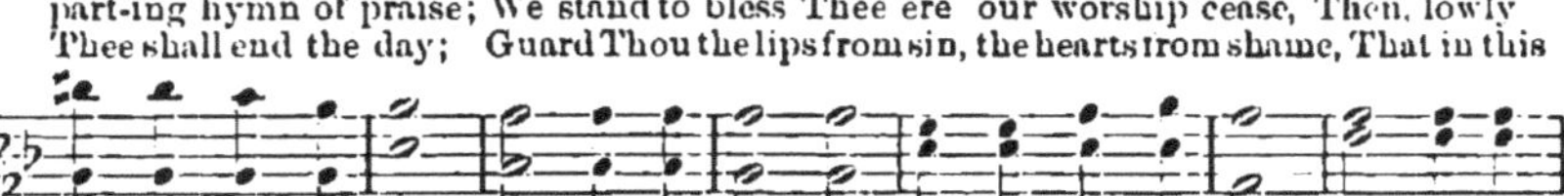
part-ing hymn of praise; We stand to bless Thee ere our worship cease, Then, lowly
Thee shall end the day; Guard Thou the lips from sin, the hearts from shame, That in this

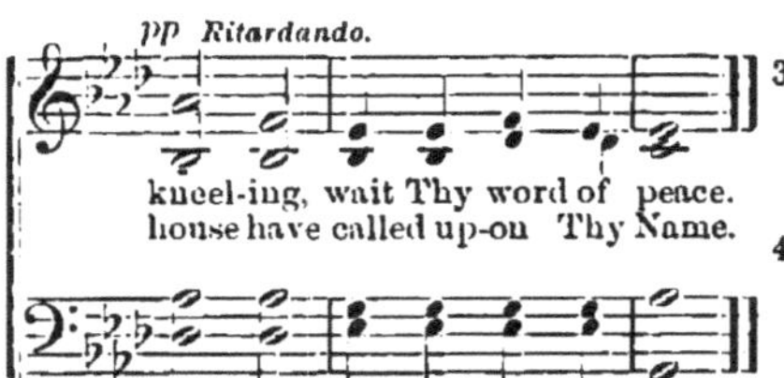
pp Ritardando.
kneel-ing, wait Thy word of peace.
house have called up-on Thy Name.

3 Grant us Thy peace, Lord, thro' the coming night,
Turn Thou for us its darkness into light;
From harm and danger keep Thy children free,
For dark and light are both alike to Thee.

4 Grant us Thy peace throughout our early life,
Our balm in sorrow, and our stay in strife;
Then, when Thy voice shall bid our conflict cease,
Call us, O Lord, to Thine eternal peace.

Art Thou Weary?

Rev. John Mason Neale, D.D. Sir H. W. Baker, har. by H. P. M.

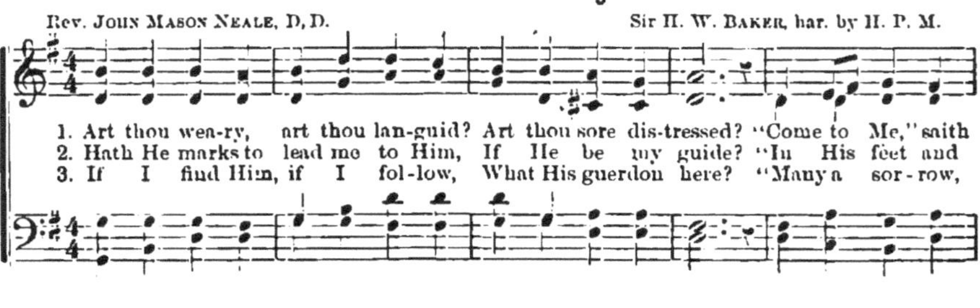
1. Art thou wea-ry, art thou lan-guid? Art thou sore dis-tressed? "Come to Me," saith
2. Hath He marks to lead me to Him, If He be my guide? "In His feet and
3. If I find Him, if I fol-low, What His guerdon here? "Many a sor - row,

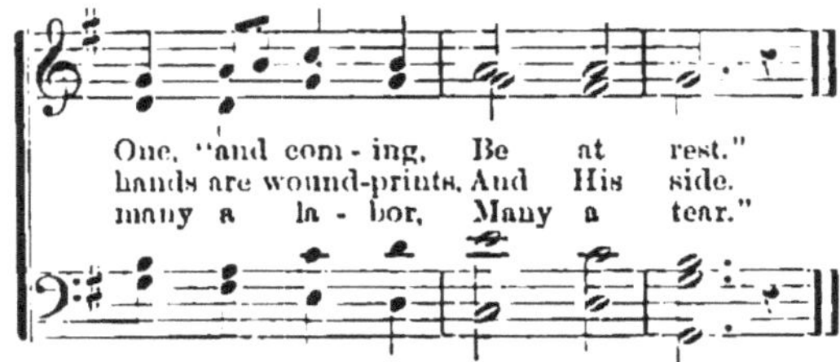
One, "and com - ing, Be at rest."
hands are wound-prints, And His side.
many a la - bor, Many a tear."

4 If I still hold closely to Him,
What hath He at last?
"Sorrow vanquished, labor ended,
Jordan past."

5 If I ask Him to receive me,
Will He say me nay?
"Not till earth and not till heaven,
Pass away."

INDEX.

Titles in Small Caps.—First Lines in Roman.

A. PAGE

A, B, C, Song ... 139
Abide with me! fast falls the Eventide... 212
A Boat, a Boat to Cross the Ferry... 73
All by the Shady Greenwood Tree... 172
Alpine Song... 61
And now, before we part... 83
Art Thou Weary?... 214
As the Moon Shone Bright and Fair... 101
Autumn is Sighing Around Me... 141
Awake! the Starry Midnight Hour... 85

B.

Blue Bells of Scotland... 118
Bye, Baby, Bye!... 97
By Killarney's Lakes and Fells... 138

C.

Cheerily, Lightly Row... 64
Chick-a-dee... 166
Closing Hymn... 214
Come and see the ripe fruit falling... 137
Come, Come, Follow, Follow... 111
Come, Gentle May... 66
Come forth this dawning early... 80
Come hither, come hither thou bird... 102
Come, let us Learn to Sing... 73
Come, Schoolmates with Me... 100
Come, Soft and Lovely Evening... 125
Cradle Song... 127

D.

Day by Day the Manna Fell... 211
Distant Chimes, (The)... 201
Dream of Home, (The)... 76

E.

Early Morning... 80
Evening Bells... 90
Evening on the Lake... 119
Evening Song... 145
Eventide... 212

F.

Fairy Greeting... 195
Faithful and True... 192
Farewell, Dear Home... 140
Farewell to the Forest... 200
Farewell to Winter... 190

G.

Gay Little Dandelion... 156
Give Welcome to the Swallow... 104
Gloria Patri... 209
Glory be to the Father... 209
God of my Life... 209
God Speed the Right... 81
Good Morning... 117
Good Night... 83
Good Night, Dear Friends... 156
Gracefully down, quietly down... 98

H.

Hail our Country's Natal Morn... 112
Hail to the Queen of Night... 60

PAGE

Hallelujah! praise the Lord!... 210
Hark! the Merry Christ Church Bells... 69
Hark! the Summer Birds... 53
Hark! what Mystic Sounds... 161
Hear the Warbling Notes... 91
He who would Lead a Happy Life... 131
Home... 194
Home, Dear Home... 126
Home Returning... 171
Home, Sweet Home... 131
Home where my young life... 194
How bright and clear the snow... 122
How merry the life of a bird must be... 150
Hurrah! welcome the day... 61

I.

I am a Lily... 52
I am Dreaming... 96
I come, I come with a bounding heart... 126
I dreamed that afar I had wandered... 77
I have a secret, 'tis ever so sweet... 132
I love to roam through forest bowers... 168
I Love to Sing... 54
In days that are sunny... 63
In Heavenly Love Abiding... 212
In my own Sweet Native Vale... 148
In Thy Lonely Path Descending... 84
I would not be a fairy light... 148
I would that my Love... 178

J.

Jack and Gill... 151
Jennie Lee... 182
Jolly Boys... 124
Joy! Joy! Now we are Free... 157

K.

Katie's Blushes... 116
Katy Did! Katy Did'nt... 78
Killarney... 138

L.

Last Rose of Summer... 130
Let the Hills Resound with Song!... 162
Light and Gay... 99
Like the Lark... 62
Little Bo Peep... 187
Little Vale with Fairy Meadows... 184

M.

Memories of Childhood... 168
Merrily Gliding On... 109
Merry May... 86
Merry waters, leaping, flowing... 95
Mid pleasures and palaces... 131
Morning Bells... 127
Morning in the Alpine Vale... 110
Morning's Ruddy Beam... 74
My Ain Sailor Laddie... 142
My Country 'tis of Thee... 175
My Dog Dash... 149
My Far-off Home... 70
My Saviour Dear... 211

N.

PAGE

Nancy Lee........ 168
Night........ 66
Night! Lovely Night!........ 55
No, No, No!........ 167
Not a link of love is broken........ 208
Now brightly on the yielding wave........ 119
Now the Day is Gone........ 133
Now the Moon is Gleaming........ 153
Now to heaven our prayer ascending........ 81

O.

Of all the wives as e'er you know........ 188
Oh, forest, deep and gloomy........ 200
Oh, I'd be a Fairy........ 186
Oh, my poor heart is breaking........ 142
Oh, Holy Saviour........ 213
Oh, the sports of childhood........ 134
Oh, the sweet summer time........ 128
Oh, Katie darling, why hide your blushes?........ 116
Old Hundred........ 210
Old John Cross........ 129
On Alpine Heights........ 152
Open wide the doors, sing aloud for joy........ 190
O sing with Voices clear and strong........ 145
O Songs of the Beautiful........ 136
O sweet evening hour........ 103
O sweet, O sweet when first the sun........ 173
O There's Music in the Waters........ 68
Our Father, who art in heaven........ 209
Our Songs of Joy and Gladness........ 196
Over the Hill the Day Light is Dying........ 159
O where and O where is your Highland........ 118
O wipe away that Tear, Love........ 79
O Ye Tears!........ 112
O! Ye Voices Gone!........ 147

P.

Parting Song........ 208
Pastorale........ 173
Praise God from whom all blessings flow........ 210

R.

Rain-Drop Chorus........ 154
Rain on the Roof........ 108
Return to School........ 183
Roaming........ 118

S.

Sabbath Morn........ 176
Saviour, again to Thy dear name........ 214
See, as morning light is beaming........ 110
See! the Morning is Breaking........ 51
Shout and sing, for soon will come........ 185
Sighing for Thee........ 120
Sit up erect, don't be afraid........ 73
Sleep, baby, sleep........ 127
Sleep, my Darling........ 123
Snow is Falling........ 56
Soft and Low........ 75
Softly roam, gentle night........ 88
Somebody's Coming........ 132
Song of the Brook........ 95
Soon to our Homes we shall Journey........ 191
Sound the Battle Cry........ 181
Star of the Evening........ 107
Sweet and Low........ 111
Sweet Evening Hour........ 103
Sweet is the Hour........ 175
Sweet Summer Time........ 128
Sweet the Pleasures........ 76
Swinging 'neath the Old Apple Tree........ 134

T.

Teacher and Scholars........ 73
Tell me, pretty little elfin........ 78
The Autumn Glee........ 137
The Bell Doth Toll........ 127
The Bird Carol........ 150
The Coming Spring........ 185
The Daisy........ 116
The Distant Chimes........ 201
The Dream of Home........ 76
The evening bells sound clearly........ 145
The Falling Snow........ 98
The Last Rose of Summer........ 130
The Lord's Prayer........ 209
The maple trees are tinged with red........ 158
The Merry Harvest Moon........ 146
The moon is up, the winds are still........ 109
The Old Black Cat........ 82
There is a flower, a little flower........ 116
There is a school of jolly boys........ 124
The Snow Birds........ 113
The Sleigh Ride........ 122
The Song of the Bee........ 63
The Song of the Cobbler........ 65
The Spring Bird........ 102
The Spring-Time is Coming........ 89
The Sweet Voice........ 77
The Village of the Vale........ 184
This beautiful morn, so bright and clear........ 117
This is the Sabbath morn........ 176
Those Evening Bells........ 130
Thou that once on mother's knee........ 211
'Tis a lesson you should heed........ 184
'Tis the last rose of summer........ 130
To school and its pleasures again........ 183
Try, Try Again........ 184
Twenty little chick-a-dees........ 166
Twilight is Stealing........ 155

U.

Under the Snow Drops........ 135
Universal Chorus........ 210
Up and down o'er hills and meads........ 118

V.

Verdant Fields........ 160

W.

Wake up Littte Daisy........ 87
Wandering up and down one day........ 65
We Tune our Happy Voices........ 114
When by others urged to tread........ 167
When down the hills, the little rills........ 154
When Mary was a Lassie........ 158
When the humid showers gather........ 108
When winter winds are blowing........ 113
Where is my Boy To-night?........ 174
Where is my wandering boy to-night?........ 174
Where the Sparkling Waters Play........ 92
Where the Warbling Waters Flow........ 57
While verdure crowns our native hills........ 86
While we sing, light and gay........ 99
Who has not felt how sadly sweet........ 76
Who so full of fun and glee........ 82
Winning every bird and blossom........ 182

Y.

Ye come, and we bid you welcome........ 195

www.ingramcontent.com/pod-product-compliance
Lightning Source LLC
Chambersburg PA
CBHW030819270326
41928CB00007B/813

* 9 7 8 3 3 3 7 3 4 9 3 3 2 *